D1365916

More Than the Blues?
Understanding and Dealing With Depression

More Than the Blues?
Understanding and Dealing With Depression

ISSUES IN FOCUS TODAY

Eileen Lucas

 Enslow Publishers, Inc.
40 Industrial Road
Box 398
Berkeley Heights, NJ 07922
USA

http://www.enslow.com

For Travis and Brendan, for our journey; for John, who brought me sunshine; and for Mary, who helped me see this through.

Library of Congress Cataloging-in-Publication Data

Lucas, Eileen.
    More than the blues? : understanding and dealing with depression. / Eileen Lucas.
      p. cm. — (Issues in focus today)
    Summary: "Examines depression and mood disorders, including the causes of depression, a history of the illness, the various types of mood disorders, and treatment methods"—Provided by publisher.
    Includes bibliographical references and index.
    ISBN-13: 978-0-7660-3065-7
    ISBN-10: 0-7660-3065-2
    1. Depression, Mental—Juvenile literature. I. Title.
    RC537.L776 2010
    616.85'27—dc22

                2008039144

Printed in the United States of America

10 9 8 7 6 5 4 3 2 1

To Our Readers: We have done our best to make sure all Internet Addresses in this book were active and appropriate when we went to press. However, the author and the publisher have no control over and assume no liability for the material available on those Internet sites or on other Web sites they may link to. Any comments or suggestions can be sent by e-mail to comments@enslow.com or to the address on the back cover.

♻ Enslow Publishers, Inc., is committed to printing our books on recycled paper. The paper in every book contains 10% to 30% post-consumer waste (PCW). The cover board on the outside of each book contains 100% PCW. Our goal is to do our part to help young people and the environment too!

Illustration Credits: BananaStock, pp. 19, 26, 80, 97; reproduced from the *Dictionary of American Portraits,* published by Dover Publications, Inc., in 1967, p. 15; iStockphoto, pp. 5, 59, 67, 82; Library of Congress, pp. 12, 62, 87; Photos.com, pp. 5, 7, 41, 44, 70; Shutterstock, pp. 3, 5, 17, 21, 29, 33, 37, 48, 53, 57, 73, 78, 84, 93, 99, 101; Stockbyte, p. 90.

Cover Illustration: Shutterstock (large photo); BananaStock (small inset photo).

Contents

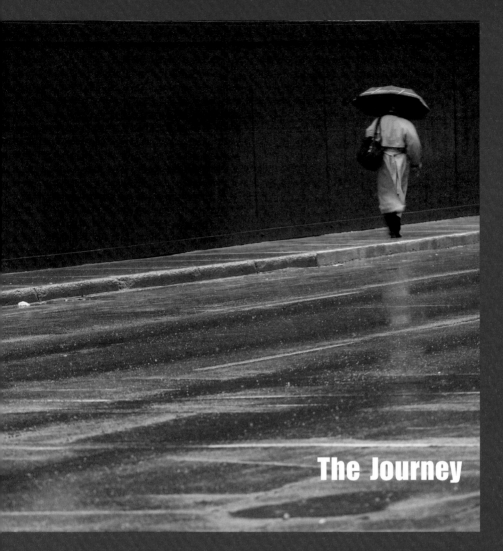

The Journey 1

One February afternoon, a seventeen-year-old high school student named Jesse called his mom at work and in a trembling voice said, "I need to talk to you tonight." When his mom got home they sat together in the family room, and with tears running down his face, Jesse explained that he felt that he could not go on. He said that it hurt too much to be alive, that he did not feel as if he cared about anything, even things he knew he enjoyed, or at least, he used to. He felt really tired, and he had no energy to do anything, but he could not sleep. He said he'd been feeling this way for a while, but he had tried to pretend that everything was okay. He could not pretend anymore.

The next day, Jesse stayed home from school, and his mom began trying to find help for him. She talked to someone at a psychiatrist's office who gave her some advice, but the psychiatrist could not see Jesse for a few weeks. After a few more phone calls, she found a counseling center that would see him that day. Jesse did not like the counselor, so the session did not go well, but Jesse talked a little about his feelings, and it was a first step.

The next step was a trip to the family doctor a few days later for some tests to rule out a physical cause for the way Jesse was feeling, such as a thyroid deficiency, or mononucleosis. The tests were negative. The family doctor called the psychiatrist's office and helped get Jesse in to see her a little sooner. In the meantime, Jesse stayed in his room, unable to go to school.

Once at the psychiatrist's office, things moved quickly. Although he had not done anything to hurt himself, Jesse was having thoughts of suicide. The psychiatrist felt that Jesse should go to a hospital where he could be watched to make sure he did not hurt himself and where he could begin to get some help for his depression.

That same night, Jesse checked in to a psychiatric hospital. It turned out that his stay there would be short; it wasn't what he needed, but he learned that only by going there. He was able to go home and, with the help of medication, return to classes, finish his senior year, and graduate from high school.

That doesn't mean that a complete turnaround happened overnight. Jesse had a bad reaction to the first medication that was prescribed for him. Another drug that helped him feel more motivated, combined with medicine to help him sleep, worked better for him. Still, there were some very dark days for a while. He did not feel good about himself and life. He tried going away to college that fall but was unable to concentrate and dropped out after a month. The journey through depression was going to take time.[1]

What Is Depression?

This is one young man's story. There are countless others. They vary in their details. As each individual is different, so is the experience of depression, but there are some common threads. Depression comes in many shapes and sizes and occurs more often than many people think. In fact, it is said to be the most common mental health disorder, so prevalent that it has been called the common cold of mental illness. It is generally estimated that about 20 percent of the population, two out of every ten people, have experienced depression serious enough to be considered depressive disorder. In the United States, depression accounts for more people out of work and in bed than any other disorder except heart disease.[2]

> **Depression occurs more often than many people think. It is so prevalent that it has been called the common cold of mental illness.**

Depression is common, but it is also serious. It has been linked to other illnesses, including heart disease. Researchers have found that people who are depressed are more than twice as likely than others to develop high blood pressure, a major cause of heart disease. Even medium levels of anxiety and depression have been associated with a 60 percent greater likelihood of developing high blood pressure. A study found that depressed people are four times more likely to have a heart attack than those with more positive states of mind.[3] In addition, people who are depressed are more likely to smoke, which is another cause of heart disease and other serious health problems.

The greatest threat is the risk of suicide. Many people who are seriously depressed admit to having suicidal thoughts at some point, and all too many act on those thoughts.

Another way to look at the seriousness of depression is to consider some of the costs connected with it. The U.S. government estimates the cost of antidepressant medications at $12.4 billion per year. The government also estimates that about $23.8 billion is lost by businesses each year due to employees being unable to work because of depression.[4]

So what is this thing called depression? The answer to that question is complicated. Some say depression is a physical illness; some say it is a psychological condition. Many say it depends. Sometimes it's mostly physical. Sometimes it's mostly psychological. Sometimes it's both. There may be several different kinds of depression with a combination of characteristics of both physical and mental illnesses, or disorders.

For the purposes of this book, depression is defined as an illness or disorder that includes physical, emotional, and behavioral symptoms such as changes in eating and sleeping patterns, overwhelmingly negative thoughts or feelings of hopelessness, and inability (or limited ability) to participate in activities that normally bring pleasure. When some combination of these symptoms lasts for an extended period of time (at least two weeks and often much longer), results in significant personal distress, and interferes with normal functioning, depressive disorder is a likely diagnosis.

Depressive disorder is in a category of illnesses known as mood disorders. It is called by many names. Sometimes it is called major depressive disorder (MDD), unipolar disorder (as opposed to bipolar disorder, described in chapter six), clinical depression, or affective disorder (*affective* means having to do with emotions).

The word *mood* describes feelings that affect our attitude toward ourselves, our behavior toward others, and our ability to get work done, to relax, or have fun. When good things happen to us, we usually react by being in a good mood. When we experience a lot of problems, disappointments, or losses, it is normal to be in a bad mood. Our mood tends to be a reaction to what happens to us.

So depression is what happens when an individual's mood response is not "normal." It is more than feeling sadness or even grief. Sadness that comes from loss is a normal part of everyone's life. Everyone has felt down about something; everyone has experienced the hurt of having best friends move away or decide they don't like us anymore. First relationships with a boyfriend or girlfriend usually end. Perhaps a beloved pet or a family member dies. Sadness is a natural human response to such situations, but that sadness is normally felt for a limited period of time and, gradually, people are able to return to a good mood.

This book is about what happens when those feelings of "bad mood" reach the level of disorder or illness, when the depressive state cannot be attributed to a particular loss, when it is out of proportion to a loss, or when the state goes on and on. This book is also about what can be done about depression. The good news is that many individuals are being successfully treated for depressive disorder. They go to school and work; they get on with their lives.

And that, ultimately, is the purpose of this book: to help readers understand depression, recognize it in themselves or others, and learn how and where to find help.

Looking Back

Depression and other mood disorders are not new. Countless individuals throughout history have struggled to lead successful lives while dealing with depression. Among them have been ordinary men and women as well as great leaders and thinkers, including American President Abraham Lincoln and British Prime Minister Winston Churchill. Abraham Lincoln was haunted by dreams and thoughts of death and dying. Winston Churchill referred to depression as a "black dog," always waiting and watching him.

Our understanding of depression and related illnesses has changed and developed over time. The ancient Greek storyteller Homer explained mental disorder as what happened when the

British prime minister Winston Churchill suffered from bouts of depression, which he referred to as a "black dog."

gods took away a person's ability to think clearly. Hippocrates of ancient Greece described an illness called "melancholy" that included physical and emotional problems caused, in part, by having too much of what was called "black bile." The Greek philosophers Socrates, Plato, and Aristotle thought that mental disorder had more to do with philosophy, or thinking about thinking, than medicine. They suggested that keeping at a distance from life's emotions was the best way to deal with what we call depression.

In the Middle Ages in Europe, many aspects of life, including the treatment of illness, were closely connected to the teachings of the Church. Mental disorder was often seen as the work of evil beings. During the time known as the Renaissance, as writers and thinkers rediscovered ancient Greek ideas, there was a renewed interest in the Greek idea of melancholy. Numerous mental and physical illnesses were grouped together under the label melancholy. Even though knowledge of how the body and brain work was very limited, doctors of that time understood that episodes of melancholy could recur and worsen over time. They knew that melancholy causes premature aging, that some forms of melancholy emerge in old age, and that melancholy leads to heart problems.

William Shakespeare, an English Renaissance author of plays and poems, wrote about some depressed characters. Hamlet, prince of Denmark, is one of the best known. At the beginning of the play *Hamlet*, the prince's inky black cloak gave the sixteenth-century audience a clue to his mood. The people of London knew that the character was depressed, although they did not use the term depression in those days.

In the 1700s, doctors in England experimented with using small amounts of electricity to shock the brains of depressed patients. The stories of Benjamin Franklin's experiments with lightning in colonial America are well known, but less well known is that he was shocked into unconsciousness (and experienced brief memory loss) during one of his electricity experiments. As a result, he is said to have recommended electric shock for the treatment of mental illness.[5]

Another one of America's founding fathers, Benjamin Rush, a doctor who was also a signer of the Declaration of Independence, understood that there was a connection between the body and the mind. He argued that the mentally ill should be treated with respect, which was not often the case in those days. Rush received money from the state of Pennsylvania to improve care for mental patients. He believed in talking with patients to understand their illnesses. His book *Medical Inquiries and Observations Upon the Diseases of the Mind,* published in 1812, earned him the title "father of American psychiatry."

In the early 1900s, the German psychiatrist Sigmund Freud began developing his theory of mental disorder. He believed that mental disorder arises from repression, or trying to hide or push away unwelcome or painful thoughts. Freud believed that repression is governed by the unconscious mind, thoughts that most people are not even aware of. According to Freud, too much repression leads to mental illness. Recovery, Freud believed, comes from examining the experiences of childhood through a process he developed and called psychoanalysis. In psychoanalysis, a patient lies on a couch and talks to the doctor about feelings and memories. Freud's views influenced the way mental illness was treated for many years. Eventually, however, a growing number of people thought that the therapy took too long, cost too much, and produced little success, so new theories came along.

In the meantime, a treatment called electroshock therapy became a fairly common treatment for depression and other psychological disorders. As delivered in the mid-1900s, this treatment could be rough on the patient. Development of new and better antidepressant medications and psychological

Dr. Benjamin Rush, known as the father of American psychiatry, argued for humane treatment of the mentally ill.

therapies led to a decline in its use and improvements in the treatment of mental disorders.

For example, in the 1940s, a drug called Thorazine (chlorpromazine) was developed to treat schizophrenia, a devastating mental illness in which the patient is often out of touch with reality. The success of this drug in treating a psychiatric disorder brought hope that medicines could help treat illnesses of the mind.

In time, more successes were recorded. Researchers found links between body chemistry and mood. In the 1950s, research by Swiss scientists led to the discovery of imipramine, a drug with antidepressant (depression-reducing) effects.

To create an organized way of explaining mental disorders, an organization of psychiatrists called the American Psychiatric Association created a document called the *Diagnostic and Statistical Manual of Mental Disorders*. This manual, known as the *DSM*, was first published in 1952. It described 106 categories of mental disorders and was 130 pages long. As additional studies were done and new ways of thinking about mental illness developed, the *DSM* was revised. New editions were published: *DSM-II*, *DSM-III*, *DSM-III-R*, *DSM-IV* and, most recently, the *DSM-IV-TR*, published in 2000. In that edition, there are approximately three hundred disorders covered in more than eight hundred pages.

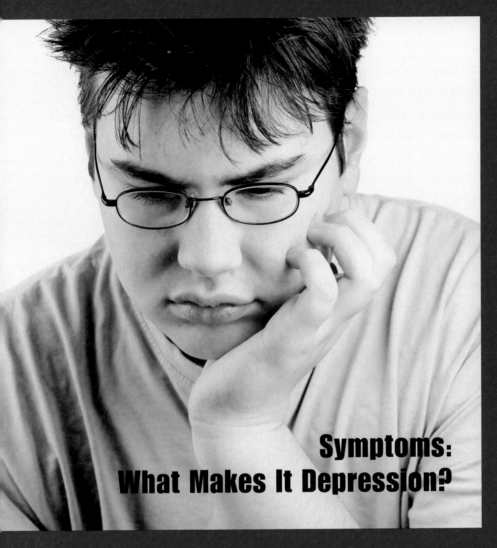

Symptoms: What Makes It Depression?

How does depression feel to someone who has it? How does it look from the outside? Those might seem like simple questions, but depression is complex and variable. It can be difficult to pin down. Sometimes an episode of depression is so dark and dramatic that no one can miss it. In other cases, it might seem to creep along, just enough to keep a person feeling down most of the time, but not unable to function. As one sufferer said, it can be "like having a constant low-grade fever."[1] People with depression describe a world drained of color, where life seems stale and empty. Problems are overwhelming, and there doesn't seem to be any light at the end of the tunnel.[2]

Just as the symptoms of various illnesses can be mistaken for the flu or a cold, the symptoms of depression have at times been confused with those of attention deficit disorder, drug and alcohol abuse, and other such complex problems. Our understanding of depression and these other disorders continues to develop. All these factors and others contribute to a many-layered description of depression.

Depression is generally considered a syndrome; that is, it includes a variety of symptoms. Not every individual diagnosed with depression experiences all the symptoms, but each has some of them. Sometimes the symptoms of depression are grouped by how they affect us: cognitive (how we think), behavioral (how we act), physical (how our body functions), and emotional (how we feel).

People with depression describe a world drained of color, where life seems stale and empty. There doesn't seem to be any light at the end of the tunnel.

Cognitive symptoms may include mental confusion, difficulty concentrating, extremely negative thoughts such as being highly self-critical, and perhaps thoughts of death. Depressed people may think about things that did not concern them before they were depressed. Many find themselves having the same disturbing thoughts again and again; these types of thoughts are known as obsessions.

Behavioral symptoms may include things that people do, such as crying a lot, as well as things avoided. For instance, a depressed person may not want to participate in activities that would normally be enjoyable.

Physical problems may include extreme tiredness and sleep problems (including both wanting to sleep all the time or not being able to sleep much at all) and weight changes related to eating a great deal less or a great deal more than normal. Physical problems can also include pain not explained by injury.

The emotional symptoms of depression are perhaps the most

familiar: feelings of extreme sadness, hopelessness, irritability, panic, guilt, and anger. These feelings do not readily go away. Sometimes, however, the feeling most associated with severe depression is a huge emptiness, a lack of strong feelings about anything, a numbness, a feeling of nothingness. As one woman said, "When I became depressed, I had no emotions at all. I always delighted at spring before. But when I was depressed, I could look at the blooms and know it was beautiful, but I had no enjoyment of it." After she started taking medication and her depression began to lift, she said, "I just started feeling again."[3]

Many people reading about these symptoms might recognize feelings that they've had. Everybody experiences some of these symptoms at some time. Bad things happen, and we react to them. The factors that separate depressive illness from the normal ups and downs of life are the intensity of the symptoms,

One of the physical symptoms of depression is fatigue.

Healthcare Specialists

Specialist	MD?	Description
General practitioner (GP) or family physician	Yes	A doctor who is generally considered a primary care physician; the person patients see for general illness and preventive care
Psychiatrist	Yes	A doctor who specializes in diagnosis and treatment of mental and emotional illness
Psychologist	Maybe	Mental health care provider trained in psychology; may have a doctoral degree (PhD), but most likely is not a trained medical doctor (MD)
Counselor	No	A National Certified Counselor (NCC) has a graduate degree in counseling and experience in settings such as marriage and family or addiction treatment

how deeply we experience them, how much they interfere with life, and how long they last.

So how does a person know if what he or she is experiencing is truly depressive disorder? A person who suspects a broken bone can get an x-ray to know for sure if it is broken and decide what to do about it. For depression, as with most psychiatric disorders, there is, unfortunately, no quick and easy x-ray or lab test to show for sure what is wrong. Many of the symptoms overlap with the symptoms of other illnesses or conditions, and a diagnosis depends on what the patient can report and what a healthcare professional (and perhaps friends and family of the patient) can observe.

Depression is often accompanied by such physical ailments as headaches.

Diagnosis

One of the first steps in finding out if a person with symptoms has depression is to choose a healthcare professional to diagnose, or label, the problem. There are several different kinds of professionals to choose from, but the diagnostic process generally includes seeing someone who is a medical doctor, or MD. General practitioners, family physicians, and psychiatrists are all MDs. That means that, among other things, they can prescribe medicine, if needed. A medical doctor can rule out illnesses that might look like depression, such as multiple sclerosis, over- or underactive thyroid, or mononucleosis. A family doctor who already knows the patient is a good place to start. If more intensive care is needed, the family doctor can then recommend a specialist.

A psychiatrist is a medical doctor who specializes in the treatment of illnesses involving emotion, behavior, and mental functioning. Persons studying to become psychiatrists go to medical school first and then continue with their education to learn about the diagnosis and treatment of psychiatric illnesses.

Because there is no simple laboratory test to tell if someone has depression, the psychiatrist has to gather a lot of other information to help make a diagnosis. He or she asks about the patient's family medical history. Mood problems in relatives can help make the diagnosis of a mood disorder more likely. Questions and answers about the patient's mood, appetite, daily activity levels, and sleep habits help with the diagnosis. The psychiatrist also asks about the patient's relationships and about how the individual is getting along with others.

Psychologists usually have an advanced degree called a PhD, which gives them the title of doctor, but usually they are not MDs, or medical doctors. In some states, individuals need only a bachelor's degree or master's degree in psychology to be called a psychologist. Because psychologists are not medical doctors, they cannot prescribe medicine, order lab tests, or perform

Some of the Questions That Might Be Part of a Medical History

- Has depression been diagnosed and treated in this individual before?
- Have relatives been treated for depression?
- What physical and emotional symptoms have been experienced?
- How long has the individual been feeling this way?
- How severe are the symptoms? How much do they interfere with daily life?
- Are thoughts about death or suicide present?

physical exams. A psychologist focuses on what is going on in the mind of the patient rather than on an illness.

The Diagnostic Process

In cases of mental and emotional disorders, just as in physical illness, an accurate diagnosis helps determine the best treatment. That's where the *DSM*, the *Diagnostic and Statistical Manual of Mental Disorders* described in chapter one, comes in.

The *DSM* places disorders into categories and groups of categories. One of the categories is mood disorders. Depressive disorders are found in this category. Other mood disorders include bipolar disorders, mood disorders due to a medical condition, and mood disorders due to substance abuse. These other types of mood disorders will be discussed in chapter six.

There are several kinds of depressive disorders listed in the *DSM*. These include:

- major depression
- dysthymia (a more chronic or ongoing form of depression, generally not as severe at all times as major depression, but usually lasting longer)
- depressive disorder NOS (not otherwise specified).

Some doctors think that some people experience depression

DSM Symptoms of Depression

- Feelings of extreme sadness or a feeling of emptiness
- Inability to enjoy things that used to give pleasure
- Sharp change in appetite
- Sharp change in sleeping patterns
- Extreme tiredness and lack of energy
- Feeling worthless or helpless
- Feeling hopeless or pessimistic
- Difficulty concentrating
- Frequent unexplained aches and pains, headaches, and stomachaches
- Thoughts of death or suicide that keep coming back

that is a blend of these categories. Major depression is what we generally mean when we talk about serious depression or depression as an illness or disorder.

According to the *DSM-IV-TR*, the most recent edition of the *DSM*, 10–25 percent of women and 5–12 percent of men will experience an episode of major depression at some point in their lives, as defined by the symptoms shown in the table.[4]

Not every individual with depression has all these symptoms, but to be diagnosed with major depressive disorder (MDD) according to the *DSM*, an individual must have at least five symptoms most of the time for a period of two weeks or longer. To be diagnosed with dysthymia, fewer symptoms may be present, and they may not be present as much of the time, but they must have been felt for two years or more.

Although we usually think of the feelings of sadness as the most obvious signs of depression, sometimes another symptom sends a person to the doctor only to find depression at the root of the problem. According to data collected by the World Health Organization, of nearly twenty-six thousand people who had seen a doctor, 69 percent of those diagnosed with depression based on the *DSM* criteria reported only physical, not emotional, problems. In other words, physical discomfort prompted them to seek medical help. Eleven percent did not report any psychological symptoms even when asked about them.[5] Perhaps they did not want to talk about emotional symptoms or maybe physical symptoms bothered them most.

Who Gets Depression?

Depression affects people of both genders as well as people from many different social and cultural backgrounds. It occurs in the very young, the very old, and every age group in between.

Children. Many people are surprised to learn that even very young children can suffer from depression. A study conducted in 1982 found that of three thousand children, nearly 15 percent showed symptoms of depression; by age fifteen, the proportion reached 20 percent (the same as in the general population).[6]

Like everyone else, most children react with sadness when something goes wrong at home or school. When children have the blues, their sad feelings usually begin to lessen within a few days. If their sadness increases or lasts for more than two weeks, or if other symptoms of depression develop, the situation may call for outside help. Depression in children should not be ignored because a child who experiences serious depression is at greater risk for having additional episodes later in life, and for developing other problems, such as uncontrollable fears, or phobias.

Another problem is that young children may not have the vocabulary to describe their changes in mood, and they may have trouble getting help. A concerned adult noticing dramatic changes in behavior can sometimes be the key to the diagnosis of depression in children.

Adolescents/teens/young adults. It is common for first episodes of depression to appear during the teenage years, often

First episodes of depression often occur in adolescence. It is estimated that one fifth of high schoolers experience some kind of psychiatric problem, such as depression.

between ages fifteen and nineteen. According to some surveys, approximately 20 percent of high school students experience some kind of psychiatric problem, including depression.[7]

Because even under the best of circumstances the teenage years can be difficult, it can be all too easy to mistake the symptoms of depression for ordinary teenage problems. (Jesse had to tell his mom straight out how badly he was feeling for her to know.) And, like young children, adolescents may find it difficult to put their feelings into words, further complicating the situation. Behavioral changes may be the most prominent symptoms, but again, virtually all teenagers try out different behaviors from time to time. Some behaviors, though, such as substance abuse, extreme risk taking, or violence (towards themselves or others), are always causes for concern.

Teenage depression that goes unnoticed and untreated can be very dangerous. According to some statistics, suicide is the third leading cause of death in persons under age twenty-five.[8] The risk of depression leading to suicide will be discussed in chapter seven.

Men and women. Both men and women can experience depression, but women tend to be diagnosed with it more often. There may be several reasons. Some experts believe women experience depression more often because of physical factors, such as changes in chemicals in the body called hormones. Others feel that the different ways men and women are taught to deal with emotions in our culture explain differences in depression in men and women. Some see other factors, such as poverty or abuse, as being important. Depression may be the result of such traumatic life events.

One kind of depression unique to women is what is often called "the baby blues," or postpartum depression. Within a couple of days after having a baby, some women experience crying spells and a feeling of unexplained sadness. That feeling seems directly connected to the hormonal changes in a woman's body following pregnancy and childbirth. Thankfully, in most cases, the feeling passes without harm. But in a very small percentage of cases, the feeling may be a symptom of a more dangerous form of the illness called postpartum psychosis. That form can cause serious problems for the mother and baby. In some cases it has been linked to the mother harming her child.

The elderly. Some people seem to expect older persons to be depressed, since our society typically places less value on this time of life. And in fact, a great many older Americans do suffer from depression. Experts estimate that up to 20 percent of the more than 30 million people over age 65 in the United States may be experiencing major depression.[9] Doctors stress, however, that depression does not have to be a normal part of aging.

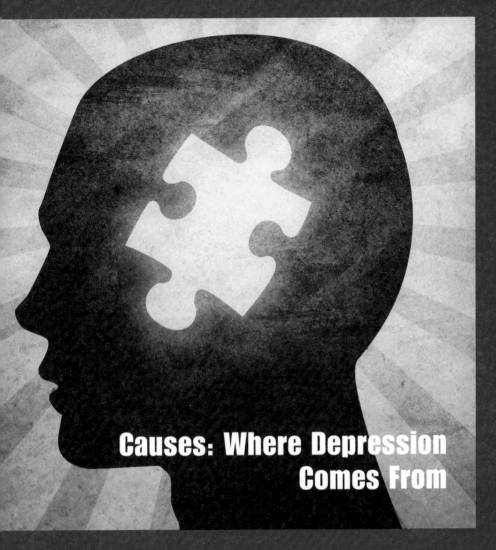

Causes: Where Depression Comes From

What causes a person to fall into depression? Sometimes it develops gradually over time from roots that go far back in a person's life. Other times it comes as a dramatic, sudden change in how a person feels. Most often, depression seems to worsen over time and, without treatment, it can last for months or sometimes much longer.

Research has shown that once someone experiences a major depressive episode, he or she is at increased risk of experiencing depression again. In other words, depression tends to recur. Approximately 80 percent of individuals who have had one episode of diagnosed depression will have more, and the risk for experiencing a new episode of depression has been found to increase by 16 percent with every additional episode.[1] In fact, when many people seek help for depression, doctors find that the patient has experienced this problem in the past.

Theories about the origins of depression continue to change, and those involved in the research and treatment of depression continue to debate them. Most experts believe that no single cause explains all cases of depression. Instead depression results from a combination of physical and psychological factors, and the particular combination of those factors varies from person to person.

Often a serious loss or unpleasant experience seems to trigger an episode of depression, but the actual cause is more complex. Something in that individual's personality, heredity, or biology "sets the stage" for depression. One or more of those factors may come into play for any particular case of depression.

Sometimes the onset of depression is compared to the way we catch a cold. We are told not to go outside in a cold, wet rain or we might catch a cold, although we know that viruses cause colds, not weather. But going out in a cold, wet rain and getting chilled just might "trigger" a virus to make us sick. In a similar way, a devastating loss might be a trigger that brings on a case of major depression.

The Neurotransmitter Connection

Scientists know that different parts of the brain play different roles in the way we think, feel, and behave. Something that goes wrong in one part of the brain can change the particular kind of thinking, emotion, or behavior that is linked to that part of the brain. For the last four decades of the twentieth century, researchers studied brain chemistry for clues about what was happening in the brain of a depressed person. This research led to the development of a theory linking depression to certain brain chemicals called neurotransmitters. Neurotransmitters are messenger molecules; they are important in the process of communication between cells in the brain.

The brain and the rest of the nervous system have been compared to a large collection of electric or telephone wires, or to a complicated network of computers. In the brain, electrical signals travel along nerve fibers till they reach the end of that cell. A chemical messenger carries the signal across the space at the end of each nerve to the next one. This messenger is the neurotransmitter. Neurotransmitters move across the space between nerve cells and match up with the surface of the next cell. Then the electrical signal continues down the next nerve cell. And on and on. Once the neurotransmitter's work is done, it either gets absorbed into a nerve cell or is broken down by other chemicals that "clean up" the space between the cells.

Researchers have concluded that mood changes may be the result of changes in the amounts of neurotransmitters in the brain. If there isn't enough of the right kind of neurotransmitters, messages can't pass between nerve cells, and communication in the brain slows down. One result of this lack of communication in the brain might be an episode of major depression.

Research has shown that depression tends to recur. Approximately 80 percent of individuals who have had one episode of diagnosed depression will have more.

There are many different kinds of neurotransmitters, but the ones that seem to be most closely linked to depression are norepinephrine, serotonin, and dopamine. Studies from the 1960s and 1970s noted that certain drugs that reduced the amount of serotonin and norepinephrine in the brain could result in depression in some individuals. Medications that increase levels of these neurotransmitters seem to decrease depression.

The theory that the kinds and amounts of neurotransmitters in the brain are directly related to depression is called the monoamine hypothesis of depression. (Neurotransmitters are in a chemical group called monoamines.) It is one of the most heavily studied theories of depression. By itself, however, the monoamine hypothesis does not answer all questions about the cause of depression. Some new antidepressant medications have little effect on the level of neurotransmitters and yet relieve depression. And some other drugs, which are known to impact neurotransmitters, have not been successful in the treatment of depression. And even if the theory is correct, it is a mystery why the level of neurotransmitters in the brain can rise quite quickly, but the beneficial response to drugs generally takes at least two weeks to become evident.

Other Physical Causes

There are other theories about how things happening in the body can affect mood and perhaps cause depression. Studies have looked at the connection between hormones in the body and depression. The neurotransmitters norepinephrine, serotonin, and dopamine play a part in the release of hormones; and hormones, in turn, affect the activity of neurotransmitters. Deficiencies in certain hormones have been associated with dramatic mood changes. Doctors have often noticed that people who suffer from diseases of the thyroid and adrenal glands, which produce hormones, have many symptoms similar to those of depression. (Thyroid malfunction was one of the first things Jesse was tested for.) Stress can cause the release of hormones that may act in some way to cause depression.

Another line of research looks at parts of the brain that are involved in higher-order thinking and emotional processing: the prefrontal and limbic regions. These regions are highly interconnected by networks of nerve cells. Studies have looked at how malfunctions in these connections can result in the symptoms of major depression.

Scientists continue to study every aspect of the brain as well

Even young children can experience depression. Theories about the causes of depression have changed over time as researchers learn more about how the brain works.

as interactions between the brain and other systems in the body to find answers. Results have yielded some very interesting information, but there are still many questions to answer.

Genetics/Heredity

Some families have more people with depressive disorder than others. This observation has led researchers to look for genetic causes for depression.

Genetics is the study of inherited characteristics. An Austrian monk named Gregor Mendel performed some famous experiments in the 1860s that showed that some traits, such as color in garden peas, seem to be determined by a single pair of genes. This is called a simple inheritance pattern. Some human traits, such as blood type, follow such simple inheritance patterns. Most human traits, however, seem to be determined by a combination of several or many genes. Depression is likely to fall into this category because, while there does seem to be some connection between genetics and depression, family history is not an automatic predictor. In other words, just because a parent has depression doesn't necessarily mean the children will as well. Instead, depression and other mood disorders fall into the category of inherited traits for which only rough estimates can be made about the chances of inheriting the disorder.

For example, individuals who have what's called a first-degree

What Are a Person's Chances of Inheriting Depression?

Relatives: Close relatives of persons diagnosed with depression have a 15 percent chance of inheriting major depression.

Twins: If one identical twin has depression, the other is 67 percent more likely to be depressed as well.

Substance abuse: If someone has relatives with depression who abuse alcohol or drugs as a symptom of their depression, that person is eight to ten times more likely to do the same.[3]

relative, such as a parent or brother or sister, with major depression are one and one-half to three times more likely as the general population to also have major depression. Up to 25 percent of those with major depression have a relative with a mood disorder of some kind.[2]

This does not mean that genetics or heredity causes depression, but rather that inheritance predicts increased risk. It does mean that people with a history of mood disorders in their families should not hesitate to seek help if they see symptoms of depression or other mood disorders in themselves.

Psychological Theories

There is also evidence that depression can develop from psychological causes. Psychological trauma experienced in childhood can have an effect on a child that results in depression then or later in life. (Jesse's father died when Jesse was ten years old. His episode of major depression occurred when he was seventeen.) Research has found that early adversity may disrupt the development of social and personal coping skills. This loss of personal resources, in turn, can increase vulnerability to depression.

Reduced personal resources. Among the personal resources that may be reduced and related to increased risk of depression are mastery and self-esteem. Mastery refers to whether people believe that they have control over the situations in which they find themselves. The degree to which a person feels in control has a big impact on how he or she copes with a situation. Mastery helps individuals handle stressful situations or avoid them in the first place. People who believe that problems are caused by outside forces beyond their control are likely to experience more stress. As a result, they may not even try to solve problems that come up in their lives. "Why bother?" they may think. Children who grow up in highly stressful home environments tend to perform poorly in school compared to other children. There seems to be a link between a difficult childhood and an inability to improve one's life.[4]

Self-esteem is a concept familiar to most people. It includes how individuals look at themselves as well as how individuals compare themselves to others. Certain circumstances in children's lives can directly reduce self-esteem and predict later mental health outcomes. Researchers have found that children who are abused physically, mentally, or sexually are more likely to have poor self-esteem and mental health problems as they grow up.[5]

Situations of adversity that go on and on throughout childhood and adolescence may be interpreted as evidence that individuals cannot change the difficult situations of their lives.

> People with a history of mood disorders in their families should not hesitate to seek help if they see symptoms of depression in themselves.

Strong evidence links these feelings of helplessness with the symptoms of depression. Support from parents and other family members can help reduce the negative impact of childhood adversity. But if the family is the source of the adversity, or if the adversity is the loss of family (through death or divorce, for example), then a child may face insurmountable obstacles. Stopping the downward path that begins with a childhood of adversity can help pave the way to a happier life.

Distorted thinking. Sometimes depression develops in the absence of childhood trauma. In these cases, distorted or mistaken patterns of thinking may have developed through ordinary living.

Then, when there is a loss or traumatic event, these distorted thoughts lead to problems. If someone loses something important to them, such as a job or a relationship, and blames himself or herself unfairly for what happened, depression may be the

A traumatic event such as the death of a loved one can sometimes trigger an episode of depression.

result. The fact that others may place no blame on the person for the setbacks often makes no difference.

The age at which the combination of loss and distorted thoughts strikes can have a big impact. If a great loss, combined with unfair self-blame, occurs at an early age, before a child has developed good coping behaviors, the stage may be set for trouble. Early loss of a parent and childhood health problems may predict later episodes of depression. Romantic break-ups are sometimes associated with the onset of first episodes of depression in adolescents—a result, perhaps of a fragile self-image at this time in life that makes negative thoughts directed inward more common.

Studies have consistently shown that people who experience significant negative life events are more likely to suffer from depression.[6] But it is not necessarily the reaction to negative life events that is the problem, but rather the "reaction to the reaction." In other words, grief following the loss is not the problem, but how a person copes with the grief is. If coping involves distorted thinking, depression may develop.

Avoidance. Depression often develops when, after a loss of some type, negative feelings are turned inward against the person who has suffered the loss. That can lead to a behavior called avoidance, and avoidance can lead to depression.

Avoidance is when a person avoids, stays away from, or denies something that causes distress. For example, if you play with matches and burn yourself, you will (hopefully) learn that playing with matches is harmful, and you will avoid that behavior due to its consequences. The behavior that is maintained then is NOT playing with matches. This is functional avoidance. It is good for you; it helps you survive.

At other times avoidance is dysfunctional, and it is not good for you. This can lead to mental disorders such as anxiety disorders and depression. For example, people who experience phobias, extreme fears of things not generally considered harmful, often exhibit avoidance behavior that can have negative consequences. An example is a fear of cars so extreme that a person cannot stand to get in one to go anywhere. Avoidance becomes dysfunctional when its long-term consequences are negative or harmful. Depression may be brought on by dysfunctional avoidance behaviors, including avoiding activities that would help combat the depression.

Negative thoughts. A related idea to distorted thinking is a concept called negative thinking, a tendency to attribute problems unfairly to weaknesses in oneself that are considered permanent and unchangeable. In other words, the individual decides that he or she is a "failure" or a "loser," and that nothing can be done about it. This type of thinking can lead to an inability to cope, hopelessness, and depression.

Some individuals find that one particular negative thought haunts them day and night when they are having a depressive episode. This same thought does not bother them at other times. It is amazing to see how these "mountains" shrink to their true "molehill" size as the depression lifts.[7] People may find it hard to believe how upset they were by that thought once they feel better. Sometimes people can tell that an episode of depression is about to begin when a particular thought or set of thoughts starts bugging them.

Depression and Sleep Disorders

There is a complicated connection between depression and sleep disorders. Some people become depressed first and then develop sleeping problems. In other cases, difficulty sleeping leads to depression. Trying to figure out which came first can help determine which symptoms to treat first.

The National Sleep Foundation conducted a poll in 2006 called Sleep in America. The poll, which focused on children aged eleven to seventeen, found that among adolescents who reported being unhappy, 73 percent reported not sleeping enough at night.[8] (In Jesse's case, his difficulties with sleep and his changes in mood are strongly connected. Two years after his episode of depression, he's still trying to develop normal sleep patterns, and he is hopeful that when he does, his difficulties with depressive mood will ease.)

Seasonal Affective Disorder (SAD)

In recent decades, experts have found that some people are more likely to be depressed at certain times of the year. Those times have been found to vary with changes in sunlight levels that come with the seasons, so the disorder is called seasonal affective disorder, or SAD. (Remember, "affective" refers to emotions.)

Typically, SAD is diagnosed when an individual experiences a strong connection between a change in mood and a particular time of the year, and the change happens two years in a row plus a third year previously. The most common form of the illness is depression in winter and normal mood in summer, but the reverse pattern is true for some people and is still considered to be SAD.

As many as 12 million Americans may suffer from this disorder, and up to 35 million others may experience milder forms.[9] It is more common in women than in men. Some estimates suggest that as many as half of all women in northern states experience SAD.

SAD comes with all the symptoms of depressive disorder but with some variations. For example, with SAD, both appetite and need for sleep usually increase, while persons with non-light-related depressive disorder might eat and sleep very little. (But these changes can go either way in both kinds of depression.) At the same time, persons with SAD generally experience the same kinds of feelings of guilt, hopelessness, and ongoing lowering of mood that accompany depressive disorder.

Not everyone enjoys cold winter days. Some people have seasonal affective disorder, or SAD, which is depression linked to variations in light at different seasons.

Symptoms Caused by Illness

A number of illnesses can cause the symptoms of depression, probably because those diseases cause the same changes in the brain as depression does. Patients experience more than being sad for being ill; they are ill and have the symptoms of depression as well.

Addison's disease is one such illness. In Addison's disease, something causes the adrenal glands to shrink. As a result, levels of the hormones that are secreted by these glands fall, which, in turn, can produce weakness, loss of appetite, weight loss, and other symptoms common to major depression.

Mood is also closely tied to the workings of the thyroid system. Hypothyroidism results from a decrease in the hormone produced by the thyroid gland. Persons with hypothyroidism often show many of the symptoms of major depression.

The glands discussed here, the adrenal and thyroid, are regulated by the pituitary gland which, in turn, receives signals from a part of the brain called the hypothalamus. Because all these systems are interconnected, problems with the pituitary and hypothalamus can also lead to depression.

Other illnesses can also include a seriously depressed mood as part of their symptoms. Parkinson's disease and Huntington's disease have devastating effects on the brain, and patients with those diseases can sometimes have episodes of major depression in the course of their illness. Multiple sclerosis, a disease of the nervous system, can cause dramatic mood changes.

Infections have also been linked to depression. Tuberculosis (an infection of the lungs), hepatitis (an infection of the liver), and mononucleosis (a viral infection that causes extreme tiredness), are often accompanied by depression. Lead poisoning can cause the symptoms of depression, too.

If so many diseases share symptoms with major depression, how do we know when the diagnosis should be depressive disorder and not some other illness? First of all, major depression is more common than these other illnesses. If a person has the symptoms of depression, depression is the most likely cause. Also, if the problem is actually one of the other diseases, other symptoms generally provide the doctor with clues. Those clues can lead to tests that confirm the diagnosis of some other illness.

Symptoms Caused by Medications

Some people develop depression as a result of taking certain medications. Some of the drugs that have been linked to depression include sleeping pills, diet pills, birth control pills, and medications for high blood pressure, arthritis, ulcers, and seizures.

Steroid medications can cause severe mood changes. Because

they are valuable anti-inflammatory agents (acting against inflammation or irritation in the body), steroids have many uses in medicine, including treatment for joint and lung diseases as well as some kinds of cancer.[10] (Steroid medications referred to here should not be confused with anabolic steroids, commonly known as performance-enhancing drugs. Anabolic steroids are sometimes used by athletes to build muscle artificially and to improve athletic performance, a practice that is neither legal nor safe.) Patients who take steroid medications should be alert for the symptoms of developing depression.

Steroids can cause mood changes in either "direction"—that is, they can cause either depression or the wild upward mood swing called euphoria. In fact, steroids can cause moods to swing first one way and then the other. When first started on a steroid, a patient may experience a state of high energy and happiness. That may last for a few days until the good feelings gradually slip away and depression sets in.

Treating Depression with Medication

4

Once depression is diagnosed, a variety of treatment options are available. Different kinds of healthcare professionals provide different kinds of treatments. For some people, understanding and dealing with the thinking patterns involved in depression are the most important parts of getting better. These patients might choose to see a psychiatrist, psychologist, or therapist to focus on psychological treatment. We will look at those treatments more closely in chapter five.

For others, the answer lies in finding out if there is something wrong with the way their brain chemistry is working. Once a good physical exam has ruled out another kind of illness as the problem, a medical doctor can offer treatment for depression with medication. A family doctor or general practitioner may prescribe an antidepressant, medication specifically for depression. Or the doctor may recommend a psychiatrist who can make the decision about antidepressant medication. A psychiatrist is a medical doctor (MD) who specializes in care related to behavioral and emotional illness.

The key is to understand that help is available. While finding the right doctor and right treatment takes time, many people, perhaps as many as 80–90 percent of those who seek help for depression, can be successfully treated, usually within three to four months.[1]

Antidepressants

Increased understanding of how the brain works has led to the development of medications to help it work better. Some of those medications help ease the symptoms of depression. In chapter three we looked at how an imbalance in certain chemicals called neurotransmitters seems to be related to the symptoms of depression. The chemicals that help fix this imbalance and ease the symptoms of depression are called antidepressants.

There are a number of different groups of antidepressants and a variety of medications in each group. The various groups tend to act on the brain in different ways. A doctor prescribing an antidepressant tries to match the needs of the patient with the right kind of medication.

Finding the right medication for a particular individual is not always easy. Doctors have a wide range of antidepressants to choose from, and the first one selected may not work. Sometimes a medication can cause new symptoms, called side effects, that can make the patient feel worse. Some studies show that the response rate to the first recommended antidepressant is somewhere around 50 percent.[2] A response does not necessarily mean that the depression goes away; it means only that the patient experiences at least some improvement. Many antidepressant medication statistics refer to this standard—that there is some improvement—and do not mean that depression is "cured."

The table on the next page shows some of the kinds of antidepressants available today. Each of these groups is examined more closely later in this chapter. Tricyclic antidepressants were among the first developed. They treat depression by boosting the level of several different neurotransmitters in the brain (including norepinephrine, serotonin, and dopamine). They block the reabsorption of neurotransmitters back into the neuron that released them. SSRIs are similar, except that they focus on one neurotransmitter, serotonin. MAOIs destroy enzymes responsible for breaking down neurotransmitters; that's how they increase neurotransmitter levels. All of the antidepressants can be effective in decreasing the symptoms of depression, such as feelings of hopelessness and extreme sadness, poor sleep and appetite, difficulty concentrating, lack of energy and interest, and so on.

Generic and Brand-Name Drugs

There are so many types of medications that keeping the names straight can sometimes be confusing. There are two basic types of drugs: brand name and generic. The brand name of a drug is the name given to it by the company that first manufactures it; the name begins with an uppercase letter, like other proper nouns. The generic name of a drug begins with a lowercase letter, and it is the name of the drug's chemical formulation. For example, the generic drug fluvoxamine has the brand name Luvox.

In the United States, a new drug can be sold only by the company that invented it as long as the patent lasts (usually between seven and twelve years). After that time, generic versions of the drug can be made and marketed by other pharmaceutical companies. Generic drugs have the same active ingredients as the original drug but are cheaper.

Examples of Antidepressant Drugs

Kind	Generic name (brand name)	Description
Tricyclics	amitriptyline (Elavil, Endep, Vanatrip) desipramine (Norpramin)	Block the reuptake, or absorption, of several neurotransmitters
SSRIs	fluoxetine (Prozac) paroxetine (Paxil) sertraline (Zoloft)	Prevent the reuptake, or absorption, of the neurotransmitter serotonin
MAOIs	moclamine (Manerix) Phenelzine (Nardil)	Block enzymes (chemicals) that break down neurotransmitters
Others	bupropion (Wellbutrin) nefazondone (Serzone) venlafaxine (Effexor)	Affect brain chemistry in different ways

Many people wonder how long they will have to take an antidepressant. These medications generally work for as long as they are taken; while they're in an individual's system, they affect the chemicals in the brain in a way that decreases the symptoms. That means that if an individual stops taking the medication, the symptoms of depression are likely to return, especially if the drug has been used for a short while. Whatever was causing the depression in the first place is still there. If medications are taken for a long enough time, however, the chemical imbalance or whatever led to the depression may have passed before the drug is discontinued.

In cases of major depression, medication is typically taken for about six months before a doctor suggests reducing the dose. If the symptoms return, the patient can go back to the original dosage. If the patient continues to feel better, then perhaps that episode of depression has passed. For milder but longer-lasting forms of depression, a doctor may wait a year before reducing the dose.

Many doctors feel that a patient should not stop taking an antidepressant too soon. Studies have shown that as many as 70 percent of patients on antidepressants become depressed again if they stop taking their medication within five weeks of having the depression lift.[3] Those who continue taking the antidepressant for at least five months after their symptoms decrease are much less likely to have the depression return.

When it *is* time to stop taking the antidepressant, doctors generally recommend a gradual reduction to avoid unpleasant side effects, such as restlessness and anxiety.

Sometimes people worry about becoming addicted to a drug that they take for a long time. Antidepressants are not addictive.

Following a thorough exam to rule out another kind of illness, a medical doctor can offer treatment for depression with medication.

They can, however, cause side effects, some of which are minor annoyances, but some of which can be quite serious, depending on which neurotransmitters are affected and how they are acted upon. Some common side effects of antidepressants include sleepiness or insomnia (difficulty sleeping), dry mouth, constipation, and dizziness. Sometimes the side effects can be lessened by taking the medication before bed (unless the side effect is insomnia!). As Dr. Francis Mark Mondimore, author of *Depression, the Mood Disease*, states, "Side effects do not mean you must stop taking the drug. Rather, it means you have a decision to make: Am I willing to put up with the side effects of this medication to get the antidepressant effect?"[4]

Sometimes a second drug is combined with the first, reducing the amount needed of each and lessening side effects. Some research indicates that about 66 percent of individuals with depression respond to a single antidepressant, and nearly 95 percent respond to a combination of antidepressants.[5] (Remember, this is a response, not necessarily a complete recovery.)

Antidepressants Are Not for Everyone

Use of antidepressants has increased dramatically in the last few decades as newer medications have been developed that have fewer side effects and as studies indicate the effectiveness of the medications. Some people find this increased use worrisome, especially because the prescribing of antidepressants for children and adolescents has also increased. Whether antidepressant medication for the young is a good thing is the subject of debate. On the one hand, few people argue with the idea of helping children with depression. On the other hand, little is known about the long-term effects of antidepressants on developing minds and bodies.

While there is also concern about the risks for pregnant women who take antidepressants, there are also concerns about serious risks for women with depression who go untreated during pregnancy. A pregnant woman who is depressed and her doctor must weigh all the risk factors and reach a decision about what is best for her and her baby.

Some people are skeptical of the effectiveness of these medications. They think that antidepressants are simply "happy pills." Researchers counter that antidepressants won't make healthy people feel a false "high" as certain illegal drugs can. If you don't have a neurotransmitter problem causing you to feel depressed, it's unlikely that taking an antidepressant will affect the way you feel.

Some therapists doubt whether antidepressants are the best way to treat depression. According to the authors of *The Myth of Depression as Disease*, "Medications are one option, but outcomes may be shorter lived than those found with behavioral therapies, and there are significant adverse side effects associated with medications."[6] Still, many individuals report that they are able to live a full and happy life with the aid of antidepressants.

Tricyclics

Before the last fifty years or so, psychiatrists treating depressed patients usually had to rely on either psychoanalysis as developed by Sigmund Freud or on electroshock therapy, which was much more traumatic at that time than it is today. In the 1950s, Swiss

Questions to Ask About Antidepressant Medications

- Why is this the best drug for me?
- What side effects are likely to occur? What can be done about them?
- Is it okay to take this with any other medications I am taking?
- What time of day should I take the antidepressant, and should I take it with or without food?
- What should I do if I miss a dose?
- How long will I take this medication before I can expect to know if it's working? How will I know?

scientists researching drugs to treat the psychological illness schizophrenia found that a medication called imipramine (sold under the brand name Tofranil) seemed to "perk up" depressed patients. It became the first of a group of antidepressants that are called tricyclics because they have a three-ring chemical structure. These drugs, plus the four-ring tetracyclics, are together called cyclic antidepressants.

Tricyclic antidepressants slow the process by which certain neurotransmitters are reabsorbed into brain cells after they do their messenger work. Tricyclics primarily block the "reuptake" of norepinephrine and serotonin, resulting in an increase in the levels of these neurotransmitters in the brain and a decrease in the symptoms of depression. Patients usually report a gradual lifting of the depression beginning within several weeks of starting the medication. Some tricyclics are taken in three or four doses daily. Others are taken in a single dose because they act on the brain differently.

Unfortunately, in the process of increasing norepinephrine and serotonin levels, the cyclics tend to interfere with other neurotransmitter systems in the brain. Their action can lead to some unpleasant side effects such as drowsiness, dizziness, and dry mouth. The side effects are dangerous when tricyclics are taken in too large a dose. These drugs may not be the best choice for individuals with certain additional psychological disorders, and people with alcohol abuse problems should avoid them as well.

For many years, these drugs were the best available for fighting depression. Today there are other choices, and tricyclics are not as commonly prescribed. In some cases though, they are still used. A physician or psychiatrist is aware of the medical conditions that may lead to problems with these medications and can help patients decide what is best for them.

Selective Serotonin Reuptake Inhibitors (SSRIs)

Drugs in the SSRI group are the ones most commonly prescribed for depression today. One in particular, known by the brand name Prozac (generic name fluoxetine), is the most popular of the SSRIs. Of the 10 million people that have been prescribed Prozac, some estimates indicate that more than 70 percent have seen improvement in their depression.[7] Other drugs in this group are Celexa (citalopram), Luvox (fluvoxamine), Zoloft (sertraline), and Paxil (paroxetine).

SSRI stands for selective serotonin reuptake inhibitor. SSRIs slow down the absorption of serotonin. After serotonin has done its work as a messenger in the brain, it is absorbed by brain cells to be used another time. This is called reuptake. When this process is slowed down, or "inhibited," more serotonin is left to send messages. Therefore, a drug that selectively inhibits the reuptake of serotonin is a selective serotonin reuptake inhibitor.

Before the last fifty years or so, psychiatrists treating depressed patients had to rely on either psychoanalysis or electroshock therapy.

These drugs seem to work at least as well as the tricyclics and with fewer side effects because they act on only one neurotransmitter. SSRIs are also used to treat other disorders in addition to depression, including obsessive-compulsive disorder (OCD), eating disorders, social phobia, anxiety or panic disorders, and posttraumatic stress disorder. SSRIs may be the safest antidepressants for heart patients because the drugs do not interfere with blood pressure or heart functioning the way some other antidepressants can.

Fewer side effects are one of the main reasons for the popularity of SSRIs, but side effects do occur. Like most antidepressants, SSRIs may cause nausea, dizziness, dry mouth, and other problems. Because these drugs are relatively new, there is some concern about the possibility of long-term effects that

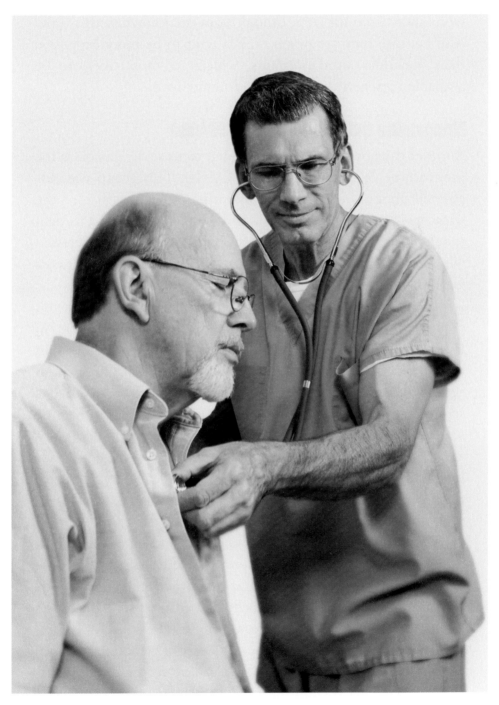

SSRIs may be the safest type of antidepressants for people with heart problems, since they do not affect blood pressure or heart function.

won't show up until later, though none are known at this time. Also because they are newer, SSRIs tend to be more expensive than the older antidepressants, which are more likely to be available in generic, or non-brand-name, form.

Monoamine Oxidase Inhibitors (MAOIs)

Another category of medications used to treat depression is the monoamine oxidase inhibitors (MAOIs). This group was discovered about the same time as imipramine, the first of the tricyclics. Drugs in this group were originally developed to treat tuberculosis, a lung disease. Psychiatrists became interested when they noticed an improvement in mood in some patients taking an MAOI for tuberculosis.

The MAOIs get their name from the fact that they act on, or inhibit, an enzyme called monoamine oxidase (MAO). An enzyme is a substance that causes a particular chemical action in the body. Monoamine oxidase is an enzyme that deactivates other amine enzymes, including the neurotransmitters serotonin, norepinephrine, and dopamine. So when monoamine oxidase is doing its job, levels of neurotransmitters are lower, and depression may be a result. MAO-inhibitor medications essentially stop monoamine oxidase from deactivating neurotransmitters, thus increasing neurotransmitter levels and providing relief from depression.

The problem is, besides having the undesirable effect of destroying the monoamine neurotransmitters, monoamine oxidase also works to eliminate another chemical called tyramine. This is a desirable effect, because tyramine raises blood pressure. When monoamine oxidase is inhibited, depression can be lifted, but blood levels of tyramine can rise, causing blood pressure to rise. That can be very dangerous.

When the MAO inhibitors were first developed, this side effect was unknown. When a number of cases of severe headaches due to a rise in blood pressure and even death from bleeding in the brain occurred in people taking MAO inhibitors, these drugs became unavailable in the United States for a number of years. Since then, they have been brought back because for some depressed people they seem to be the only medication that works. But now we know that people who take them need to be careful about what they eat, restricting their intake of foods that lead to a rise in tyramine. Some of the foods that individuals taking MAOIs need to avoid include sausages, smoked meat, cheese, some kinds of fruit, coffee, chocolate, and soy sauce.

Because of this, people who have trouble following a strict diet probably cannot take MAOIs. Individuals with high blood pressure, serious heart problems, or breathing problems related to bronchitis or asthma are not good candidates for these medications either.

Balanced against the risks are certain notable benefits. "I've seen a few miracle cures with these drugs," one psychiatrist noted. "And they're particularly good if people suffer from panic attacks in addition to depression."[8]

Other Drugs

Besides tricyclics, SSRIs, and MAOIs, various other drugs can be prescribed to treat depression. Because they are chemically unrelated to those three categories or to each other, we might call them "the unrelated drugs." They include Effexor (venlafaxine), Serzone (nefazodone), and Wellbutrin (bupropion).

Those drugs have been developed from research on the effect of antidepressants on brain chemistry. Each affects different neurotransmitters or the message communication system in the brain in a different way. For example, Effexor (venlafaxine) targets three neurotransmitters: norepinephrine, serotonin, and dopamine. Serzone (nefazodone) increases serotonin levels by slowing serotonin absorption. Wellbutrin (bupropion) fights depression by targeting norepinephrine and dopamine levels.[9]

These drugs can cause side effects similar to those brought on by other antidepressants.

Effexor is a reuptake inhibitor of serotonin and norepinephrine. Because it has a different chemical structure, some people who don't respond favorably to other antidepressants respond to Effexor.

Serzone acts in some ways as the SSRIs and the tricyclics do. Some people taking this medication report that they start feeling less anxious and can get a good night's sleep. This medication's ability to help people sleep can be beneficial for people with depression who are also agitated or who experience insomnia.[10]

Wellbutrin is another chemically different antidepressant. It is a serotonin and norepinephrine reuptake inhibitor that also affects the neurotransmitter dopamine. It doesn't cause some of the side effects of other antidepressants, but it does have one serious side effect of its own, and that is an increased risk of a seizure (a malfunctioning in the brain).

Sleep Medications

When depression is associated with sleep problems, a doctor may prescribe sleep medications. Such drugs may provide temporary relief for difficulty sleeping, and they can sometimes significantly improve mood, especially when sleeplessness is a reaction to a particular worry or situation. But researchers note that sleeping pills are not likely to help either long-term sleep problems or the depression related to them.

Herbal Treatments

For over two thousand years, the herb St. John's wort (scientific name *Hypericum perforatum*) has been used for a variety of health purposes. Hippocrates of ancient Greece and Pliny of ancient Rome used it as a medicine. In the Middle Ages, St. John's wort was used to treat depression, and in the mid-nineteenth

Hypericum perforatum, or St. John's wort, is an herb that has been used to treat depression since ancient times.

century, the Shakers, an American religious group known for their knowledge of herbs, used St. John's wort as a cure for "low spirits."[11]

St. John's wort has been studied through the years to try to discover the secrets of its healing powers. Those studies have found the plant to be generally safe, but some side effects may occur when St. John's wort is taken with certain medications, including some antidepressants. St. John's wort is very popular in Europe, particularly in Germany.

It appears that the part of the plant that gives it its reddish color is primarily responsible for St. John's wort's mood-boosting ability. This substance, hypericin, seems to interfere with the breakdown of neurotransmitters, acting in the same way as anti-depressant medications.

The U.S. National Institute of Mental Health led a study in which St. John's wort was compared with SSRIs in the treatment of depression. Patients with major depression were randomly assigned to one of three treatments: St. John's wort, an SSRI antidepressant, or a placebo. (Sometimes called a sugar pill, a placebo looks like a regular pill but does not contain any medicine.) Although all three types of treatments helped some people, researchers were not able to prove that St. Johns' wort worked better than antidepressants or a placebo for major depression. (The antidepressant seemed to be slightly more effective by some measurements.) Still, those who believe in the effectiveness of St. John's wort say that, when used daily for a month or more, St. John's wort helps mildly depressed people regain a more normal mood and attitude.[12] It is also sometimes used to help decrease the symptoms of mild anxiety and sleep disorders.

Other Treatments for Depression

Treating depression with medication is not the only option. As we've seen, depression can result from many causes, some physical, some psychological. It makes sense that a treatment will be more likely to succeed when it is carefully matched with the factors that led to the depression in the first place. When these factors are physical, such as malfunctioning brain chemistry, medication may play a role in recovery. When they are psychological, such as low self-esteem or a habit of negative thinking, a form of psychological therapy is probably appropriate. Often, a combination of both kinds of treatment may offer the best chance of relief.

Sometimes psychotherapy is the first and only form of treatment used. In cases in which depression seems to be a response to difficulties in life complicated by attitudes and behaviors that interfere with that individual's ability to cope, it makes sense that depression might be best treated by promoting changes in those attitudes and behaviors. Some researchers go so far as to say that, even if a physical problem is the cause, a medical treatment might not be the best method. With drugs, recovery might be temporary and include side effects, while psychotherapy might prove more successful and longer lasting without side effects.

A treatment for depression will be more likely to succeed when it is carefully matched with the factors that led to the depression in the first place.

A person suffering from depression may need to see more than one kind of healthcare professional to get well. An individual may see a family doctor to rule out physical illness and perhaps to get started on medication. If the person sees a psychiatrist, that doctor may be able to provide a prescription for medication (and monitor its use), while also providing psychotherapy, or psychological treatment. Or the individual with depression may see a psychologist, or some other type of counselor or therapist, for psychological help. With the popularity of medical treatment for depression, it is easy to forget that, before the many medications that are available today were developed, almost all treatment for emotional and mental illness was psychological.

There is sometimes heated disagreement about which kind of treatment is best, with some people advocating only medical care (medication), while others believe only in psychological treatment (psychotherapy). Sometimes the best of both worlds comes together, and both medical and psychological treatments are used. Medication might be used first to improve a person's mood, and then psychotherapy might be tried to change underlying beliefs and behaviors. Various combinations of treatments receive widespread support. The bottom line is that no one treatment works for everyone. Just as there are many reasons people develop depression, there can be many pathways to getting well. And getting well is the ultimate goal.

Psychotherapy

Medical illness is something physically wrong in a living being. Mental or psychological illness is something wrong in the thinking or learning of a person. Psychotherapy treats psychological illness. Because depression can be caused by thinking or learning that produces behaviors that have negative results, psychotherapy can be an appropriate treatment. Psychotherapy aims to correct the thinking or learning that is causing problems.

Psychotherapy is also sometimes referred to as "talk therapy," or counseling. Psychotherapy can be described as a conversation between two people: an individual professionally trained to gather information in a particular way and a person seeking help.[1] Psychotherapy can strengthen a person's ability to cope with life's struggles. It can help a person understand the kinds of attitudes and behaviors that lead to depression.

Psychotherapists (persons trained in psychotherapy) help patients understand how their past experiences contribute to their present attitudes and behaviors. They help patients to develop new coping skills and approach life's difficulties in more effective ways.

There are many forms of psychotherapy in use today. Many of them have their roots in psychoanalysis, the kind of psychotherapy developed by Sigmund Freud. Psychoanalysis involved the patient lying on a couch with the psychoanalyst sitting behind him or her, listening to the patient talk, helping the patient search through memories for thoughts and feelings developed in childhood that led to current problems. The

Sigmund Freud, the inventor of psychoanalysis. The form of "talk therapy" pioneered by Freud is one type of treatment for depression.

patient would generally meet with the doctor three or four times a week for an hour each time over a period of years. As you can imagine, this treatment would get very expensive, and results would take a long time. For those reasons, psychoanalysis is not a common treatment for depression today.

In the 1950s, Carl Rogers developed a new form of psychotherapy called client-centered therapy. This treatment focused on "active listening." An active listener is focused on hearing what the individual is saying and truly understanding what he or she means. The person speaking, in this case an individual with depression, is directing the conversation as they explore their thoughts and feelings. Supporters of client-centered therapy believe that this technique can give the patient as well as the doctor a clearer understanding of the problems leading to depression.

Behavior Therapy

At about the same time that Carl Rogers was developing his active listening treatment, other researchers were developing a treatment called behavior therapy. Behavior therapy uses a variety of techniques to change behaviors that cause problems, such as the following:

Relaxation training. Learning how to relax the muscles of the body deeply has been proven to help reduce anxiety.

Behavioral rehearsal. This procedure helps the patient develop specific social skills. A therapist and patient put together a plan with steps that lead the patient toward a desired goal. The patient practices the steps until he or she can use the new behavior in everyday situations.

Relabeling. How a person responds to a situation emotionally is often the result of how the situation is "labeled" in the mind of that person. Behavior therapists help patients to become aware of how they think about situations. They encourage them to test their assumptions (things that are believed to be true without necessarily having evidence to support that belief) about situations that cause them severe stress.[2]

Cognitive Therapy

Another form of psychological treatment is cognitive therapy. Cognition means thinking. Cognitive therapy is based on the idea that moods and emotions result from thought patterns. Cognitive therapy seeks to change a person's moods and emotions by changing that person's thinking.

Cognitive therapy was developed by Dr. Aaron Beck. Dr. Beck noticed that the patients who came to see him for depression all seemed to have overwhelmingly negative thoughts about themselves and life. He developed cognitive therapy as a way to treat depression by changing those negative thoughts. At about the same time, another psychologist, Albert Ellis, also developed an approach to psychotherapy that focused on cognition, or thoughts. Today a number of different forms of cognitive therapy are used to treat depression and other mood disorders.

Those who practice cognitive therapy are actively involved in the patient's treatment, asking for information and proposing possible solutions to problems. The cognitive therapist does not spend as much time looking into the past as is done in some other forms of therapy. The focus of cognitive therapy is the attitudes or assumptions individuals have about themselves and their place in the world that can lead to negative thoughts. It is these negative thoughts that are considered to be at the root of depression.[3]

The therapist helps patients recognize their negative thoughts and see the problems caused by such thoughts. Once the patient sees the connection between these thoughts and the depressed feelings they have, they can begin to replace negative thoughts with appropriate, positive thoughts.

Some examples of the kinds of thinking errors targeted by cognitive therapy include such beliefs as: "I am of little value," "I am not capable of achieving anything of importance," or "Things are never going to change for the better." The first step for the cognitive therapist is to show the patient that these beliefs are not necessarily true; that they are not based on reliable evidence. The next step is to change the patient's mistaken attitudes, replacing them with more appropriate attitudes that can result in relief from depression.[4]

Cognitive and behavioral therapy are often now combined and called cognitive-behavior therapy, CBT for short. Therapists who treat people with depression using CBT look at the ways in which people process and organize information about life. Depression is viewed as the outcome of mistaken negative beliefs. The goal of cognitive-behavior therapy is to replace negative thoughts and beliefs

> **Cognitive and behavioral therapy are often now combined and called cognitive-behavioral therapy, CBT for short.**

with more accurate and positive ones. Behavioral and cognitive techniques are used to accomplish this goal. Effective treatment involves working on the thinking as well as the behaviors that led to depression.

Many studies support the use of cognitive-behavior therapy with depressed patients. Some studies have compared the treatment of depression with CBT to treatment with antidepressant medication. One study done at the University of Toronto in Canada looked at what parts of the brain were affected by these treatments. Members of both the CBT and the medication groups experienced about the same amount of improvement. Then the scientists scanned the patients' brains. "Our hypothesis was, if you do well with treatment, your brain will have changed in the same way, no matter which treatment you received," said researcher Zindel Segal.[5]

But this was not the case. Patients' brains responded differently to the two kinds of treatment. CBT lowered activity in the part of the brain involved in reasoning and logic and raised activity in the brain's emotion center. Medication had the opposite effect. As another researcher, Helen Mayberg, explained, "Cognitive therapy targets the thinking brain, reshaping how you process information and changing your thinking pattern. It trains the brain to adopt different thinking circuits."[6]

Because CBT teaches new coping behaviors, it seems to retain its effect after treatment has ended. Some studies indicate that the changes brought about by CBT may be longer lasting than relief achieved through medication. One study went back a year after treatment to compare patients who had gone through cognitive therapy and patients who had taken medication. The researchers found that only about 31 percent of the cognitive therapy patients had relapsed, or had their depression return, after treatment was ended, while 76 percent of those who had taken medication relapsed once the medication stopped.[7]

Another plus for CBT is that it does not produce the side effects that are common with medications. Still, whether psychotherapy, such as CBT, can substitute for medical treatment is a subject of much disagreement. A more accepted belief is that antidepressant medications can work together with psychotherapy. For some patients, the relief of symptoms that can come with medication seems to be a necessary first step. As the depression begins to lift, patients may then be better able to participate in and benefit from psychotherapy.[8]

Other Forms of Psychotherapy

A number of other types of psychotherapy are also used to treat depression:

Interpersonal therapy (IPT). IPT focuses on improving personal relationships, especially relationships in which there are issues related to depression. During the first few sessions with an IPT therapist, the patient and therapist discuss various relationships in the patient's life and identify issues, such as conflicts with family or friends, and the connection of those issues to the patient's depression. In the following sessions, usually over five or six months, these issues are worked on. According to the University of Michigan Depression Center, "Several years of careful study has shown that IPT is equally as effective in the short term treatment of depression as antidepressant medication therapy."[9] For the therapy to be even more effective, monthly follow-up sessions, called maintenance therapy, may be recommended.

Additional therapies. Additional therapies include psychodynamic therapy and group therapy. In psychodynamic therapy, a therapist helps the patient try to resolve conflicts from the past to relieve depression. Group therapy uses feedback from a

People participate in group therapy led by a counselor. Many people find group therapy helpful for dealing with depression.

therapist and others who have experienced similar symptoms to ease depression. One of the key benefits of group therapy is that the patient sees that he or she is not alone; others have experienced depression and are working to overcome it.

Electroconvulsive treatment (ECT). ECT, sometimes called electroshock therapy or simply shock therapy, is poorly understood by most people. Despite the scary images that may come to mind, ECT has been very helpful to some people with depression. About one hundred thousand people are treated with ECT in the United States each year.[10]

In modern ECT, a controlled electric pulse is delivered through a padded electrode placed on the patient's head, creating a brief electrical "seizure." This seems to boost neurotransmitter levels in the brain, similar to the effect of antidepressant medications. The patient is given anesthesia beforehand, so that all muscles are relaxed, and the patient experiences none of the jumping or jerking that occurred with older methods. Some temporary memory loss may be experienced, especially for the time period right before the treatment, but significant permanent memory loss generally does not occur. Of the patients who fail to respond to drug treatment, approximately half respond to ECT.[11]

Hospitalization. The kinds of therapies that have been looked at here are usually aimed at helping persons work through and get past their depression. But sometimes the symptoms interfere so much with life that the depressed person needs to be in a hospital where care can be given around the clock. Hospitalization may be critical when thoughts of suicide have been expressed. In a hospital setting, persons feeling suicidal can be watched very carefully while they are being treated for depression.

Bright lights. As we saw in chapter three, some people become depressed when there is not enough sunlight. Some people believe that the most effective treatment for this form of depression, known as seasonal affective disorder (SAD), is light therapy. This therapy involves sitting in front of special lights that are usually about ten times brighter than normal indoor light. Usually, this is only necessary in the wintertime, when shorter days bring on depression. The amount of time needed in front of the light can vary, but for some people, four to six hours of bright light each day is required. While sitting a few feet from the lights, patients can read, sew, or do paperwork, as long as they keep their eyes open and glance directly into the light for a few seconds every minute or so. Although light therapy can be more time consuming than some other treatments and some researchers feel that evidence of its effectiveness is limited, it has few side effects.[12]

Exercise. Some evidence suggests that regular aerobic exercise (such as running, biking, or swimming) can ease the symptoms of depression by raising the level of neurotransmitters in the brain, much in the same way that antidepressants do. Even a brisk walk for ten to twenty minutes can help. A half-hour of exercise at a time, at least three to five times a week, seems most effective for improving mood.

Magnetic stimulation. This therapy, formally called repetitive transcranial magnetic stimulation, or repetitive TMS, is similar in some ways to electroconvulsive therapy (ECT), but it does not require anesthesia. This experimental therapy uses magnets to make nerve connections in the brain more efficient. Through a coil about the size of a human's hand held over the head of the patient, an electric current is generated in a targeted area of the brain.

This is a new and experimental treatment, and only a relatively small number of patients have been treated with this method so far. The benefits seem to last for around four months, at which time the treatment can be repeated. It may

Research has shown that exercise can help relieve the symptoms of depression by affecting the neurotransmitters in the brain.

have fewer side effects than medications, but it is expensive because it requires a highly technical machine operated by a skilled technician. It is available only in a few countries at this time, including Canada, Australia, New Zealand, Israel, and some countries of the European Union.[13]

Other alternative treatments. Studies have been done on various alternative treatments for depression, including therapeutic writing intervention, massage, music therapy, and nutritional therapy. Additional studies are needed to further explore the effectiveness of these and other alternative treatments for depression.[14]

Considering Treatment Options

The decision whether to choose medication, psychotherapy, ECT, some other treatment, or some combination of treatments depends on what kind of depression is involved, how much the depression is interfering with the individual's life, and a number of other factors. As author Anne Sheffield says in *How You Can Survive When They're Depressed*, "What works in one situation will not work in all; what may be useful in one case may be a waste of time and money in another, or in some instances downright dangerous."[15]

In 1989 the National Institute of Mental Health published the results of a study of 250 patients who suffered from depression. Some patients were given antidepressant medication. Some were given psychotherapy. Some were given a placebo. In cases where the depression was fairly mild, antidepressant medications and psychotherapy were about equally effective. Interestingly, neither was more effective than the placebo. For patients whose depression was severe, however, medication was the best, fastest, and cheapest treatment.[16]

Some things to consider when deciding what kind of treatment to choose:

1. Some depressions will go away on their own over time. If living with depression is not causing too many problems at home, school, or work, no medical or psychological treatment may be necessary.

2. If a specific life event or a particular behavior seems to be the cause of the depression, psychotherapy may be a good treatment option.

3. Psychotherapy may also be a good choice when the person with depression has a tendency toward negative attitudes that a trained therapist can help with.

4. A form of depression called manic depression or bipolar disorder (which will be examined in the next chapter) should always be treated with medication.

5. Treatment costs and health insurance benefits may need to be considered when deciding on a form of treatment.[17]

Other Mood Disorders

A number of other psychological conditions or disorders share some of the same symptoms with the unipolar, or major depression, that has been the focus of this book so far.

Bipolar Disorder

As if severe depression were not bad enough, for some people it is only half the story. They also experience extreme "highs," called mania. For days or weeks, they feel on top of the world—as if nothing can stop them. That might sound good, but the problem is that they are out of touch with reality. They are hyperactive, they talk too loud and too fast, they spend money they do not have, and they think strangers—perhaps even dangerous ones—are their best friends. They engage in high-risk behaviors. They may become irritable or paranoid, and then suddenly, they crash, finding themselves overwhelmed with hopelessness and guilt, swallowed up by depression.

This condition is called manic depression or bipolar disorder. It is called "bipolar" because of the two poles—periods of severe depression that alternate with periods of extreme or manic "highs." Either of these states can be severe enough to require hospitalization to keep the individual from harming himself or herself. Persons with untreated bipolar disorder are likely to experience difficulties at school and work and in relationships. They may abuse alcohol or drugs. They may be at risk for suicide.

Bipolar disorder is not nearly as common as unipolar depression. It is estimated that 1–2 percent of men and women develop bipolar disorder.[1]

Bipolar disorder is caused by a chemical imbalance in the brain. There is strong evidence that it is linked to genetics. An individual diagnosed with it often has family members with similar symptoms. This connection does not mean, however, that because one family member has this disorder, another family member definitely will. In at least some cases, certain life events can bring on the illness for which genetics has established a vulnerability.

Bipolar disorder is considered a lifelong illness to be treated rather than cured. Statistics indicate that 90 percent of those who experience both the extreme lows and the extreme highs of bipolar disorder need continued treatment for this illness. The average age when bipolar disorder begins is about twenty, and it seems to strike young men and women with equal frequency. Children and teenagers younger than twenty who have had episodes of major depression may be at increased risk for developing bipolar disorder.[2]

The good news is that effective treatments are available and, with treatment, individuals with bipolar disorder can channel their talents and abilities into productive lives. Actress Patty Duke struggled with bipolar disorder for many years before finding the treatment that would allow her to enjoy the success her hard work had earned. Dr. Kay Redfield Jamison is a highly successful psychiatrist who has used all she learned about her own manic depression to help others understand this disorder.

Three main types of medication are used to treat bipolar disorder: mood stabilizers such as lithium; anticonvulsants, such as carbamazepine, which help stop intense muscle contractions; and antipsychotic medications, such as thioridazine, which help an individual stay in touch with reality.[3]

The drug that has been used the longest for bipolar disorder is lithium. It is a mineral that is present in some soils. The early Greeks noticed that when people with what they called "melancholy" bathed in spring water that contained a lot of lithium salts, they became happier.

Today, lithium is used mostly to even out the mountains and valleys of a person's emotional swings. It can bring someone down from mania and control mood in some people. Sometimes an antidepressant is also prescribed to deal with the lows, but the drug has to be carefully monitored so that it doesn't bring on rapid changes in moods.

> Bipolar disorder is considered a lifelong illness to be treated rather than cured. Statistics indicate that 90 percent of those with bipolar disorder need continued treatment.

People on lithium need to have their blood levels tested regularly because lithium only works when it is at the right level in the bloodstream and because the difference between the right amount and enough to make a person very sick is quite small. Alcohol can cause problems and should be avoided by people taking lithium.

In recent years, a number of new medications have been

introduced to treat bipolar disorder. Zyprexa (olanzapine), Tegretol (carbamazepine), and Depakote (valproic acid) are now sometimes used instead of lithium or in combination with it.[4]

These medications are a very important part of the treatment of bipolar disorder. For many years lithium seemed to be the only choice, and if it did not work, there were few alternatives. But since these drugs are fairly new, we don't know if people who do well on them at first will continue to see that improvement after the many years of treatment that bipolar disorder requires. Only time will tell.

Anxiety Disorders

Anxiety is a normal reaction to stress. It helps people deal with challenges and work through problems. But when anxiety becomes extreme, dealing with those same problems becomes difficult. Then anxiety becomes a disorder.

Many studies have found that depression and anxiety disorders often occur together. In fact, statistics suggest that over half the people who suffer from depression also have some type of anxiety disorder.[5] Sometimes the anxiety episodes only happen when depression is present, and sometimes the two problems occur separately and follow different paths. Research continues to search out the connections between these disorders.

Anxiety Disorders

- **Panic disorder**
- **Agoraphobia**
- **Social phobia**
- **Obsessive-compulsive disorder (OCD)**
- **Posttraumatic stress disorder (PTSD)**
- **Generalized anxiety disorder (GAD)**

The box shows some of the types of anxiety disorders identified by the *DSM-IV-TR*. An individual with panic disorder might have a sudden feeling that something terrible is about to happen, along with such physical symptoms as rapid heartbeat, difficulty catching one's breath, dizziness, weakness, sweating, choking, nausea, and a tingling feeling. A panic attack can happen at any time, taking an individual completely by surprise. In fact, some people have experienced panic attacks in their sleep!

A phobia is an intense fear of something that is not obviously frightening to most people. Agoraphobia is described in the *DSM-IV-TR* as a fear of being in situations from which escape could be difficult or embarrassing. The dictionary defines it as an abnormal fear of being in crowds, public places, or open areas. It is a kind of anxiety disorder. Sometimes agoraphobia develops when panic disorder is not effectively treated.

Social phobia, also called social anxiety disorder, occurs when individuals find themselves overwhelmed with anxiety in certain situations around other people. A particular kind of situation, such as eating with others, may cause trouble, or people with social phobia may have difficulty just about any time they are in

Anxiety is a normal reaction to stress. But when it becomes extreme, dealing with problems becomes difficult. Then anxiety becomes a disorder.

public. These situations might bring on such symptoms as an upset stomach, sweating, blushing, trembling, or difficulty speaking.

People who are diagnosed with obsessive-compulsive disorder (OCD) have repeated, unwanted thoughts (these are obsessions) along with repeated behaviors (these are compulsions). The repeated behaviors, such as frequent hand washing, may be related to the unwanted thoughts, such as an excessive concern about germs.

Social phobia, which involves a fear of interacting with other people, is one type of anxiety disorder.

Posttraumatic stress disorder is that grouping of symptoms that tends to appear after an intensely negative or shocking life event. We most commonly hear about PTSD in relation to soldiers who have been in combat. It can also result from a bad accident, an attack, or a natural disaster. Persons with PTSD may experience frightening thoughts about the traumatic event, difficulty sleeping, jumpiness, uneasiness, or feelings of emotional numbness.

It is estimated that nearly 5 percent of Americans have generalized anxiety disorder (GAD), making it one of the most common anxiety disorders. Nearly two-thirds of GAD patients are women.[6] This disorder is defined by continuous, exaggerated worry that the individual cannot shake. These tense, worried feelings are often accompanied by tiredness, headache, muscle aches, sweating, and crabbiness.

"Avoidance behavior," such as staying in bed for long periods of time and avoiding activities that used to be fun, is often seen in persons with anxiety disorder. By "shutting down," the individual is "avoiding" the pain.

A link between depression and anxiety disorders has been suspected since at least the 1960s, when researchers noticed that some patients with severe anxiety symptoms seemed less anxious after being given antidepressants.[7] This treatment seemed to be most effective in patients who had attacks of anxiety separated by periods of much less anxiety, rather than in those who were continuously anxious.

Psychotherapy can be an important part of the treatment for anxiety disorder. As might be expected, when people with this disorder come up against a situation that causes them problems, anxiety begins to rise. Studies show that if the individual is able to stay in contact with the feared situation in a safe environment for long enough, the anxiety level reaches a peak and then begins to decrease. Skilled psychotherapists help their patients face the fear and work through it.

Borderline Personality Disorder

Borderline personality disorder (BPD) is a mental disorder involving extremely intense and changeable moods and emotions. Persons with BPD tend to experience intense episodes of anger, depression, and anxiety that may appear suddenly and may be accompanied by aggression towards others, acts of self-injury, or drug or alcohol abuse. They may have difficulty getting along with others, but at the same time, they may frantically try to avoid being alone.

It is believed that about 2 percent of adults have BPD, and it is more common in women than men. It often occurs together with other psychiatric problems, including major or

Depression and substance abuse often go hand in hand. People sometimes try to self-medicate through the use of drugs or alcohol.

unipolar depression, bipolar disorder, and anxiety disorders. Treatment often includes some form of psychotherapy to work on behaviors associated with this illness. Sometimes medications are prescribed to target specific symptoms. Research continues to try to understand the brain chemistry and environmental triggers that lead to BPD and to help the individuals who suffer from it lead normal, productive lives.[8]

Chemical Dependency: Alcohol and Drug Abuse

Just as major depression and anxiety disorders can occur together, major depression and chemical dependency can go hand in hand as well. Some people with mood disorders drink excessively or use other substances that bring on a "high," or euphoria, because the chemicals temporarily relieve the pain of depression. Often, however, such efforts to "treat" mood problems with drugs or alcohol set another chain of events in motion that can lead to still more problems.

Because chemical dependency can cause some of the same symptoms as depression, and depression can look a lot like chemical dependency, it can be difficult to be sure which is the root of the problem in a particular case. A leading expert on alcoholism has stated that in about 90 percent of patients who have symptoms of both alcoholism and depression, the depression is secondary to the alcoholism.[9] Sorting out the cause and effect can be a very important step in getting the right treatment.

7 **Taking Action**

Fallout is a term that refers to the consequences of an event. As author Anne Sheffield tell us in her book *How You Can Survive When They're Depressed*:

> At any given moment, approximately 17 million Americans are suffering from a depressive illness. At least the same number, and probably many more, suffer from depression fallout. They are the people closest to those with the illness: the spouses, parents and children who experience the consequences of living in close proximity to someone else's despair.[1]

One father whose daughter had severe depression described it as "being part of a funeral that never ends."[2]

In *Overcoming Depression*, authors Dr. Demitri F. Papolos and Janice Papolos state:

> When a relative experiences repeated episodes of depression or mania, there is an extremely disruptive and disorganizing effect on family life. The other members of the family are faced with the challenge of looking after and providing for the needs of their relative while at the same time maintaining their other responsibilities at work and at home—often within an atmosphere of confusion, isolation, embarrassment, anger and guilt.[3]

The Family

When the person with depression is a child, parents suffer along with their child; they are likely to wonder what the child's future will be like. Under such circumstances, the needs of other family members often go unmet.

When a family member is depressed, other family members may feel that giving that person extra attention will make him or her feel better. When the depressed person does not respond positively to attention, other family members are likely to feel frustrated, angry, or guilty. These feelings can lead to a cycle of exhaustion and negative emotions for everyone involved.

While each family's story is unique, common problems and emotions tend to arise repeatedly. With professional help, families can learn ways to cope.

The first task for each family member is to understand depression. The very idea of mental illness and the vocabulary of psychiatry and medications can be confusing, and even frightening—for the person with depression and for family and friends. An individual with depression can greatly benefit from an "ally," someone to provide support, guidance, and understanding throughout treatment. As Dr. Francis Mark Mondimore says, "What patients do not need is someone telling them to 'shape up' or 'snap out of it,' as if that's all it

When a child or teen is depressed, parents suffer along with their child, and needs of other family members may go unmet.

takes to get better. What they do need is someone who can help them get help."[4]

A fairly common misconception is that people with depression should be able to cheer up and talk themselves "out of it" on their own. According to a 1992 telephone survey by the Alliance for the Mentally Ill of Pennsylvania, 40 percent of those surveyed believed that "most people who are mentally ill could be well if they only had the will."[5] In another poll, this one by the National Institute of Mental Health, about half the people surveyed felt that depression was a "personal weakness" rather than a health problem.[6]

Actually, just the opposite is often true. Many people with depression demonstrate a great deal of strength in the face of their illness. As a social scientist who also suffers from depression, David Karp wrote in *Speaking of Sadness*, "Each interview caused me to marvel at the courage depressed people display in dealing with extraordinary pain."[7]

Whether we think of depression as a physical illness or a psychological disorder, it is not just a personal weakness, something a person should be able to get over without help. Everyone struggles to overcome the ordinary, occasional feelings of being depressed, especially as a result of one of life's many setbacks. Hardly ever can full-blown major depression be conquered

A poll by the National Institute of Mental Health found that about half the people surveyed felt that depression was a "personal weakness" rather than a health problem.

alone. That is not to say that it cannot be conquered. It means that professional help can make a huge difference.

As the author of *Depression, the Mood Disease* says, "People who are suffering from mood disorders need a tremendous amount of professional support, reassurance, and education."[8] Especially at the beginning of treatment, frequent visits to a healthcare professional may be needed. It takes time and help to get well.

Another important factor in overcoming illness is a positive attitude, a belief that help is available and treatment will work. Unfortunately, a person suffering from major depression may find a positive attitude extremely difficult, if not impossible. Hopelessness is a symptom of the illness, and efforts to get well can seem wasted, pointless.

"This is where family and friends come in," says author Dr. Francis Mark Mondimore. "They must be the source of support and optimism in treatment. I sometimes tell family members who wonder why their relative is so complaining and rejecting that 'it's the illness talking.' It's important to remember that this attitude will disappear when the illness is successfully treated. To criticize the depressed person for resisting treatment is like blaming someone with a broken leg for not being able to walk."[9]

Sometimes people with depression lack the energy to seek help. Worse still is the fear that their depression is their own fault and others will blame them for how they feel. Sadly, this can be true if family and friends do not understand depression. Too many depressed people do not get help for their disorder; they fear the label of mental illness so much that they try to hide and live with their pain. In an article in *The American Journal of Managed Care*, Aron Halfin, MD, reports that "depression remains a significantly underrecognized and undertreated condition with less than one third of adults with depression obtaining appropriate professional treatment."[10] This is due to several factors, including cost and availability of appropriate care, and something called stigma.

Stigma

One of the problems that sufferers of depression face is the stigma of mental illness. Stigma is a negative meaning or attitude attached to something. Former First Lady Rosalynn Carter, who has worked very hard on behalf of mental health

Former First Lady Rosalynn Carter has been a strong advocate for mental health care.

care, describes stigma as "the tremendous gap between what the experts know about brain-related illnesses and what the public understands."[11] Because there is so much misunderstanding about brain-related illnesses, people who seek help often face discrimination in what schools they can attend, what jobs they can get, what kind of healthcare benefits they can receive, and much more. Such discrimination is the result of stigma.

"Stigma breeds shame and silence where neither should exist," says author Anne Sheffield. "There is nothing shameful about mental illness; an illness is an illness, whether of the brain, the heart, or the lung."[12]

People with mental illness are often feared. While some

individuals with mental illness are capable of doing harm to themselves or others, according to the American Psychiatric Association, people with mental illness, like other people with disabilities, are far more likely to be victims of crime than they are to be criminals.[13]

One form of discrimination is lack of medical insurance coverage for psychiatric benefits. As difficult as it can be to get affordable healthcare for physical illness, the costs and other difficulties can be many times magnified for mental illness. Rosalynn Carter says, "I firmly believe that making insurance benefits for mental illnesses and physical illnesses the same would do more than anything to dispel stigma."[14]

Mental health care is generally treated differently by insurance companies than physical healthcare.[15] Office visits to a psychiatrist or counselor may be limited or not covered at all, and the portion of the bill paid by the insurance company may be lower. Insurance companies often place a strict limit on the number of days a patient can stay in a psychiatric hospital, and this limit can be well under the amount of time needed to get well. Mental health organizations are working to pass laws to correct this situation, but today, the lack of insurance coverage is a serious problem for many people seeking treatment.

The Ultimate Risk

Few who have not experienced it understand just how terrible the pain of major depression can truly be. Mike Wallace, former anchor of the CBS television news program *60 Minutes*, writes:

> It's difficult to make others understand how desperate a deep depression can make you feel, how lost, how cope-less, how grim. And no light at the end of the tunnel. And there is no way properly to describe the anguish that a depressive can put his family through. Gloom, doom, no love, no real communication, short temper, and leave-me-alone fault-finding.[16]

This terrible pain brings us to the most serious consequence of

Warning Signs of Suicide

- **Talk of suicide**
- **Constant thoughts of, and talk about, hopelessness and death**
- **Increased risk taking**
- **Withdrawal**
- **A new crisis for someone who was already depressed**
- **Sudden change in attitude, such as sudden calm after prolonged depression**
- **Putting things in order, "tying" things up**

untreated or ineffectively treated major depression—the risk of suicide.

Statistics vary, because some suicides may be misreported as accidents and families may want to remain silent about such a tragic event. Suicide ranks between the eighth and eleventh leading cause of death in the United States. Approximately thirty thousand Americans commit suicide each year, and for each death, about ten attempts fail.[17] According to the American Academy of Child and Adolescent Psychiatry, thousands of American teens commit suicide each year, making it the third leading cause of death for persons between ages fifteen and twenty-four.[18] Author Anne Sheffield writes that probably 90 percent of those teenagers suffered from some form of depression or other psychiatric disorder; many also had drug and alcohol problems.[19]

In a *New York Times* interview after a young person committed suicide, Dr. Thomas Jensen, head of the adolescent psychiatric unit of St. Mary's Hospital in Lewiston, Maine, said, "When you are depressed, you could have a million things going for you but if one thing is wrong, the depressed person completely loses perspective. He focuses on that one negative thing, and he convinces himself that suicide is the only option."

A boy who had thought about suicide while depressed reported later, "My God, I was so distorted. It was scary. I look back now and think, 'How could I have even thought of killing myself?' But I thought it was the only option. I know better now."[20]

Ironically, there are steps in the process of getting help for depression that can increase the risk of suicide. Sometimes severely depressed people are so withdrawn that any action, even suicide, is too much of an effort. As they begin to get better and begin to have more energy, but are still a long way from

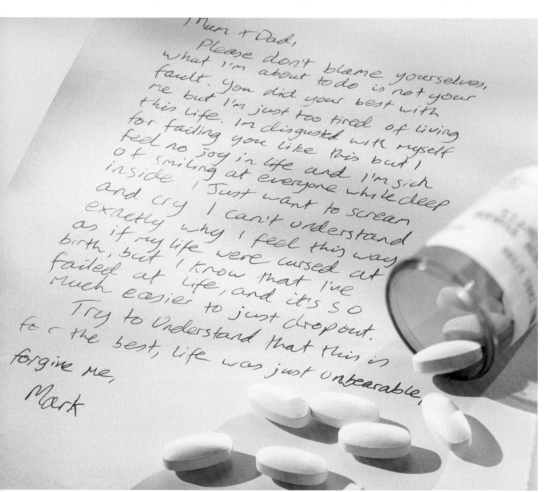

Suicide is the most serious consequence of untreated (or ineffectively treated) major depression.

well, they may have enough energy, but not enough hope, and may try to take their life.

Another frightening irony is that some studies indicate an increased risk for suicide among people taking antidepressants. These results remain very controversial, but manufacturers of antidepressants are required to include a warning about the increased risk of suicide or suicidal thinking for children or adolescents when taking these drugs.

Teens and Suicide: What to Watch For

Risk factors for teenage suicide include the following:

- People who have made previous attempts at suicide may try again, especially during the first months after an unsuccessful attempt.

- Teens who have been hospitalized for psychiatric care have an increased risk of suicide.

- Teens who talk of being a failure and see themselves as unable to meet the high standards of themselves or others may be at risk for suicide.

- A recent loss may leave a vulnerable teenager so lost and alone that suicide seems the only option.

- Some teens abuse drugs or alcohol to deal with the pain of depression, and this combination can increase the chances of a suicide attempt.

- A gun in the house may make it easy for a troubled teen to commit suicide. According to teen suicide expert Dr. Richard O'Connor, "If you have a gun in your home, you are five times more likely to have a suicide in your house than homes without a gun."[21]

Steps to Take When Warning Signs Appear

If someone you know exhibits warning signs:

- **Remove access to weapons**
- **Remove access to medications that could be harmful in overdose**
- **Keep the lines of communication open, especially avoiding giving the depressed person reason to put him or herself down even more**

If *you* are having thoughts of suicide

- **Call a suicide hotline or 911**
- **Go to an emergency room**
- **Tell someone you know will help you get help**

- Young people who come from families that regularly resolve conflict through violence may be at greater risk of using violence against themselves.

- Teens who have never learned the communication skills that allow for a discussion of their feelings may turn to suicide.[22]

The bottom line: If a person is feeling too low to enjoy life and these feelings keep hanging on for weeks at a time, that person should get help. Thoughts of suicide mean it is crucial to get help right away.

If a friend or family member confesses thoughts of suicide to you, *always* take the matter seriously. Tell someone who can help.

Taking Part in Getting Well

It has been said that one of the best ways to prevent suicide is to prevent the return of depression. Getting effective treatment and working until the depressed person truly feels better need to be priorities.

"There are two parts to the equation: a skilled doctor and a

While people with depression do not need to be told to "snap out of it," they can benefit from having an understanding, supportive ally.

patient who realizes that he or she also shapes the outcome of treatment," say the authors of *Overcoming Depression.* "Success very much depends on the ability of the patient to take an active part in and make a commitment to the treatment alliance."[23]

If medication is tried, the patient has to understand and accept that a period of trial-and-error can take months. If one medication does not work, time will be needed for it to clear from the patient's system before another is tried. This time of uncertainty, which may last months or even years, can be very frustrating, and the patient may become angry and may find it difficult to be hopeful.

Sometimes patients turn their negative feelings against the professionals who are trying to help them. Depressed people may stop taking the medications prescribed for them or change the amount or timing of taking medications without consulting a doctor. They may have unrealistic expectations of the doctor or therapist, and they may become disappointed or angry when their expectations are not met. They may continually miss appointments and give up on treatment.[24]

This is why it is so important for the individual with depression to recognize the choices that he or she needs to make to get well. Otherwise, as one patient puts it, "It makes it too easy for patients to take themselves off the hook of personal responsibility and to behave like victims, which is not healthy in the long run. I see it as similar to taking insulin for diabetes and then ignoring the need for an appropriate diet."[25]

Sarah Carlisle is a therapist who understands living with depression because she has the disorder herself. Carlisle knows how important it is to take her physical and emotional health needs seriously. She deals with her depression through medication, psychiatric care, yoga, and personal relationships—a combination that allows her to be successful. For her, a red flag to watch for is loss of appetite. "That's my cue that I need to pay extra attention to taking care of myself—and see my doctor if it doesn't get better. I may not ever be cured, but proper treatment keeps me feeling happy and healthy, emotionally and physically."[26]

Self-help for Coping With Depression

- Get enough sleep.
- Eat a healthy diet.
- Find ways to relax.
- Get involved in activities you enjoy or used to enjoy, even when you don't really feel like doing anything.
- Seek help at times when you feel low or face extra stress.

Tips for Coping With Sleeplessness

- Go to bed and get up at about the same time every day.
- Don't take afternoon naps if you have trouble falling asleep at night.
- Do something relaxing before bed.
- Get some exercise every day.
- Avoid caffeine and alcohol.
- Avoid large meals and beverages late at night.

Organizations That Can Help

A number of organizations can help with gaining understanding and getting help. The National Depressive and Manic Depressive Association (NDMDA) provides support and encouragement to patients and their families through support groups and educational programs. NDMDA publishes a newsletter with information about new treatments and sponsors conventions and workshops. Upon request, the NDMDA will send a list of available resources.

The National Alliance for the Mentally Ill (NAMI) started in 1979, and it has since grown into a nationwide organization with chapters in every state. NAMI members work for better access to mental health services and insurance benefits for everyone affected by mental illness. They also seek to educate family members of mental health patients and the general public about psychiatric issues.

The National Mental Health Association is another national organization with chapters all over the country. It is an excellent resource for learning about mental health issues.

Cause for Optimism

At this time, there are no cure for depression, but there are many ways to deal with and control the disorder. According to former First Lady Rosalynn Carter:

Depression is the most treatable of all the mental illnesses. With our new knowledge of the brain, diagnoses are more accurate and treatments have improved considerably, bringing relief to many who have suffered. If you or someone you care about is having symptoms that you think may be the result of depression, you should seek help from a mental health professional. There is no need to suffer unnecessarily when there is so much help available.[27]

New and better treatments for mood disorders will continue to become available. Better medications will be developed with fewer side effects. Treatments that involve such natural therapies as light, sleep, nutrition, and exercise will become more effective and reduce the need for medication. Advanced technologies for looking into the brain may help in understanding, diagnosing, and treating depression.

"Happiness comes from being fully engaged in life, from paying attention to the present moment, to the process of living," says Dr. Richard O'Connor in *Undoing Depression*.[28] Life is good. Believe it!

Chapter Notes

Chapter 1 The Journey

1. Interviews with "Jesse" (name has been changed to protect privacy), 2006–2008.

2. Rosalynn Carter and Susan K. Golant, *Helping Someone with Mental Illness* (New York: Three Rivers Press, 1999), p. 19.

3. Carol Turkington and Eliot F. Kaplan, *Making the Antidepressant Decision* (Chicago: Contemporary Books, 2001), p. 24.

4. Ibid., p. 4.

5. Ibid., p. 46.

Chapter 2 Symptoms: What Makes It Depression?

1. David A. Karp, *Speaking of Sadness: Depression, Disconnection, and the Meanings of Illness* (New York: Oxford University Press, 1996), p. 3.

2. Demitri F. Papolos and Janice Papolos, *Overcoming Depression* (New York: Harper & Row Publishers, 1987), p. 10.

3. Carol Turkington and Eliot F. Kaplan, *Making the Antidepressant Decision* (Chicago: Contemporary Books, 2001), p. xxi.

4. Lisa L. Weyandt, *The Physiological Bases of Cognitive and Behavioral Disorders* (Mahwah, N.J.: Lawrence Erlbaum Associates, 2006), p. 134.

5. Ginny Graves, "The Hidden Signs of Depression," *Self,* February 2007, p. 99.

6. Turkington and Kaplan, p. 36.

7. Ibid., p. 38.

8. Francis Mark Mondimore, *Depression, the Mood Disease* (Baltimore: The Johns Hopkins University Press, 1993), p. 120.

9. Turkington and Kaplan, p. 41.

Chapter 3 Causes: Where Depression Comes From

1. Turhan Conli, ed., *Biology of Personality and Individual Differences* (New York: The Guilford Press, 2006), p. 353.

2. Francis Mark Mondimore, *Depression, the Mood Disease* (Baltimore: The Johns Hopkins University Press, 1993), p. 158.

3. Carol Turkington and Eliot F. Kaplan, *Making the Antidepressant Decision* (Chicago: Contemporary Books, 2001), p. 26.

4. Heather A. Turner and Melissa J. Butler, "Direct and Indirect Effects of Childhood Adversity on Depressive Symptoms in Young Adults," *Journal of Youth and Adolescence* (2003), vol. 32, iss. 2, p. 89.

5. Ibid., p. 3.

6. Allan M. Leventhal and Christopher R. Martell, *The Myth of Depression as Disease* (Westport, Conn.: Praeger Publishers, 2006), p. 69.

7. Mondimore, p. 75.

8. "Depression and Sleep," National Sleep Foundation, 2007, <http://www.sleepfoundation.org/site/apps/nlnet/content3.aspx?c=huIXKjM0IxF&b=2427705&content_id={90A2192C-A80E-467B-85AD-25CA3EE85356}&notoc=1> (August 21, 2008).

9. Turkington and Kaplan, p. 28.

10. Mondimore, p. 168.

Chapter 4 Treating Depression With Medication

1. Carol Turkington and Eliot F. Kaplan, *Making the Antidepressant Decision* (Chicago: Contemporary Books, 2001), p. 42.

2. Mark A. Reinecke and Michael R. Davison, eds., *Comparative Treatments of Depression* (New York: Springer Publishing Company, 2002), p. xii.

3. Turkington and Kaplan, p. 58.

4. Francis Mark Mondimore, *Depression, the Mood Disease* (Baltimore: Johns Hopkins University Press, 1993), p. 57.

5. Lisa L. Weyandt, *The Physiological Basis of Cognitive and Behavioral*

Disorders (Mahwah, N. J.: Lawrence Erlbaum Associates, 2006), p. 150.

6. Allan M. Leventhal and Christopher R. Martell, *The Myth of Depression as Disease* (Westport, Conn.: Praeger Publishers, 2006), p. 33.

7. Turkington and Kaplan, p. 63.

8. Ibid., p. 170.

9. Ibid., p. 116.

10. Ibid., p. 122.

11. Ibid., p. 201.

12. Ibid., p. 202.

Chapter 5 Other Treatments for Depression

1. Demitri F. Papolos and Janice Papolos, *Overcoming Depression* (New York: Harper & Row Publishers, 1987), p. 140.

2. Allan M. Leventhal and Christopher R. Martell, *The Myth of Depression as Disease* (Westport, Conn.: Praeger Publishers, 2006), p. 123.

3. Francis Mark Mondimore, *Depression, the Mood Disease* (Baltimore: Johns Hopkins University Press, 1993), p. 208.

4. Anne Sheffield, *How You Can Survive When They're Depressed* (New York: Three Rivers Press, 1998), p. 113.

5. Sharon Begley, "How the Brain Rewires Itself," *Time*, January 29, 2007, p. 77.

6. Ibid., p. 78.

7. Leventhal and Martell, p. 124.

8. Carol Turkington and Eliot F. Kaplan, *Making the Antidepressant Decision* (Chicago: Contemporary Books, 2001), p. xv.

9. "Interpersonal Psychotherapy for Depression," University of Michigan Depression Center, 2003–2006, <http://www.med.umich.edu/depression/ipt.htm> (August 22, 2008).

10. Turkington and Kaplan, p. 46.

11. Sheffield, p. 96.

12. Mondimore, p. 145.

13. Michael Craig Miller, "Minds and Magnets," *Newsweek*, December 11, 2006, p. 62.

14. Lisa L. Weyandt, *The Physiological Basis of Cognitive and Behavioral Disorders* (Mahwah, N. J.: Lawrence Erlbaum Associates, 2006), p. 158.

15. Sheffield, p. 101.

16. Ibid., p. 114.

17. Ibid., p. 116.

Chapter 6 Other Mood Disorders

1. Lisa L. Weyandt, *The Physiological Basis of Cognitive and Behavioral Disorders* (Mahwah, N. J.: Lawrence Erlbaum Associates, 2006), p. 159.

2. Ibid., p. 161.

3. Ibid., p. 172.

4. Carol Turkington and Eliot F. Kaplan, *Making the Antidepressant Decision* (Chicago: Contemporary Books, 2001), p. 193.

5. Allan M. Leventhal and Christopher R. Martell, *The Myth of Depression as Disease* (Westport, Conn.: Praeger Publishers, 2006), p. 69.

6. Turkington and Kaplan, p. 118.

7. Francis Mark Mondimore, *Depression, the Mood Disease* (Baltimore: Johns Hopkins University Press, 1993), p. 151.

8. "Borderline Personality Disorder." National Institute of Mental Health, n.d., <http://www.nimh.nih.gov/health/publications/borderline-personality-disorder.shtml> (August 22, 2008).

9. Mondimore, p. 165.

Chapter 7 Taking Action

1. Anne Sheffield, *How You Can Survive When They're Depressed* (New York: Three Rivers Press, 1998), p. 1.

2. Rosalynn Carter and Susan K. Golant, *Helping Someone with Mental Illness* (New York: Three Rivers Press, 1999), p. 7.

3. Demitri F. Papolos and Janice Papolos, *Overcoming Depression* (New York: Harper & Row Publishers, 1987), p. 167.

4. Francis Mark Mondimore, *Depression, the Mood Disease* (Baltimore: Johns Hopkins University Press, 1993), p. 197.

5. Carter and Golant, p. 19.

6. Carol Turkington and Eliot F. Kaplan, *Making the Antidepressant Decision* (Chicago: Contemporary Books, 2001), p. 2.

7. David A. Karp, Speaking of Sadness: *Depression, Disconnection, and the Meanings of Illness* (New York: Oxford University Press, 1996), p. 12.

8. Mondimore, p. 83.

9. Ibid., p. 198.

10. Aron Halfin, "Depression: The Benefits of Early and Appropriate Treatment," *The American Journal of Managed Care*, November 13, 2007 (4 Suppl): S92–7.

11. Carter and Golant, p. 3.

12. Sheffield, p. 9.

13. Carter and Golant, p. 18.

14. Ibid., p. 23.

15. Mondimore, p. 223.

16. Sheffield, p. viii.

17. Turkington and Kaplan, p. 14.

18. "Teen Suicide," American Academy of Child & Adolescent Psychiatry, May 2008, <http://www.aacap.org/page.ww?name=Teen+Suicide&section=Facts+for+Families> (August 22, 2008).

19. Sheffield, p. 233.

20. Ibid., p. 234.

21. Richard O'Connor, "Teen Suicide," Focus Adolescent Services, n.d., <http://www.focusas.com/Suicide.html> (August 21, 2008).

22. Turkington and Kaplan, p. 40.

23. Papolos and Papolos, p. 162.

24. Ibid., p. 163.

25. Mark A. Reinecke and Michael R. Davison, eds., *Comparative Treatments of Depression* (New York: Springer Publishing Company, 2002), p. xiii.

26. Ginny Graves, "The Hidden Signs of Depression," *Self*, February 2007, p. 101.

27. Carter and Golant, p. 153.

28. Richard O'Connor, *Undoing Depression* (Boston: Little, Brown and Company, 1997), p. 324.

Glossary

adrenal glands—Two glands located near the kidneys which produce chemicals that help the body function and are thought to be involved in the human stress response.

adversity—Serious hardships and troubles.

affective—Having to do with emotions and feelings.

anti-inflammatory—Something that works against irritation or inflammation in the body.

avoidance—A psychological term for behavior that involves staying away from or avoiding things that are upsetting.

clinical depression—A name for depression as a disease or illness.

dopamine—A neurotransmitter that may play a role in feelings of reward or pleasure.

dysfunctional—Behavior or situations that result in negative consequences or feelings; something that does not contribute to positive functioning.

dysthymia—A chronic or ongoing form of depression; may not be as severe as major depression, but lasts longer.

electroconvulsive treatment (ECT, also known as electroshock therapy)—The use of electric current to stimulate the brain as a treatment for depression and other mental disorders.

enzyme—A substance that causes a particular chemical reaction to occur.

euphoria—An extreme feeling of happiness and well-being.

generic—Not trademarked.

genetics—Having to do with heredity or the origins of something.

hormones—Chemicals released into the bloodstream by a number of glands in the body that influence body functions and behavior.

hypothalamus—A part of the brain that connects the brain with various systems in the body.

limbic region—A part of the brain thought to be involved with emotions and behavior.

major depressive disorder (MDD)—The term for depressive disorder used in the Diagnostic and Statistical Manual of Mental Disorders (DSM). A number of symptoms need to be present to be diagnosed with MDD.

mania—An extremely intense or exaggerated enthusiasm or excitement.

mastery—In psychological terms, having a sense of being in control of, or able to deal with, a situation.

melancholy—A term used since ancient times for illnesses that include physical and emotional symptoms.

monoamines—A group of chemicals in the body that includes neurotransmitters.

neuron—A nerve cell.

neurotransmitter—A chemical that acts as a messenger between neurons.

norepinephrine—A neurotransmitter thought to play a role in attention and response.

phobia—An extreme fear, usually of something not everyone is afraid of.

pituitary gland—A small gland at the bottom of the brain that sends messages to other glands and plays a role in a number of body functions.

placebo—A substitute for real medicine in a research study; a harmless but ineffective pill given in place of real medicine to compare with the effects of the real medicine. Sometimes called a "sugar pill."

psychiatry—A branch of medicine specializing in the study of mental illness.

psychoanalysis—Form of psychotherapy developed by Sigmund Freud.

psychotherapy—Treatments that use psychology and psychological research in the treatment of mental illness.

reuptake—The absorption or elimination of a substance.

serotonin—A neurotransmitter thought to play an important role in mood.

steroid—A type of medication used in many ways; not to be confused with anabolic steroids, which are used illegally as performance-enhancing drugs by some athletes.

stigma—A negative meaning or attitude attached to something.

syndrome—A group of symptoms that occur together.

thyroid gland—A gland found in the neck that plays a role in energy levels.

tyramine—A substance found in some foods that can cause blood pressure to rise dangerously.

unipolar depression (or unipolar disorder)—Depression without the extreme "highs," or mania, of bipolar depression.

For More Information

American Foundation for Suicide Prevention HotLine
1-800-273-TALK (8255)

Depression and Bipolar Support Alliance (DBSA)
730 N. Franklin Street, Suite 501
Chicago, IL 60654-7225
Phone: 1-800-826-3632

International Foundation for Research and Education on Depression (iFred)
2017 – D Renard Ct.
Annapolis MD 21401
Phone: 410-268-0044

National Alliance on Mental Illness (NAMI)
2107 Wilson Blvd., Suite 300
Arlington VA 22201-3042
HelpLine 800-950-NAMI (6264)
Phone: 703-524-7600

Further Reading

Berne, Emma Carlson, editor. *Depression.* Detroit: Greenhaven, 2007.

Cobain, Bev. *When Nothing Matters Anymore: A Survival Guide for Depressed Teens.* Minneapolis, Minn.: Free Spirit Pub., 2007.

Irwin, Cait, with Dwight L. Evans and Linda Wasmer Andrews. *Monochrome Days: A Firsthand Account of One Teenager's Experience With Depression.* New York: Oxford University Press, 2007.

McIntosh, Kenneth. *The History of Depression: The Mind-Body Connection.* Philadelphia: Mason Crest Publishers, 2007.

Miller, Allen R. *Living With Depression.* New York: Facts On File, 2007.

Nelson, Richard E., and Judith C. Galas. *The Power to Prevent Suicide: A Guide for Teens Helping Teens.* Minneapolis, Minn.: Free Spirit Publishing, 2006.

Roy, Jennifer Rozines. *Depression.* New York: Benchmark Books, 2005.

Scowen, Kate. *My Kind of Sad: What It's Like to Be Young and Depressed.* Toronto: Annick Press, 2006.

Salomon, Ron. *Suicide.* New York: Chelsea House Publishers, 2007.

Internet Addresses

American Academy of Child & Adolescent Psychiatry
<http://www.aacap.org>

Depressedteens.com
<http://www.Depressedteens.com>

Depression.com
<http://www.depression.com>

Index